AF479022

Ellen Gallagher
Accidental Records

Hauser & Wirth Publishers

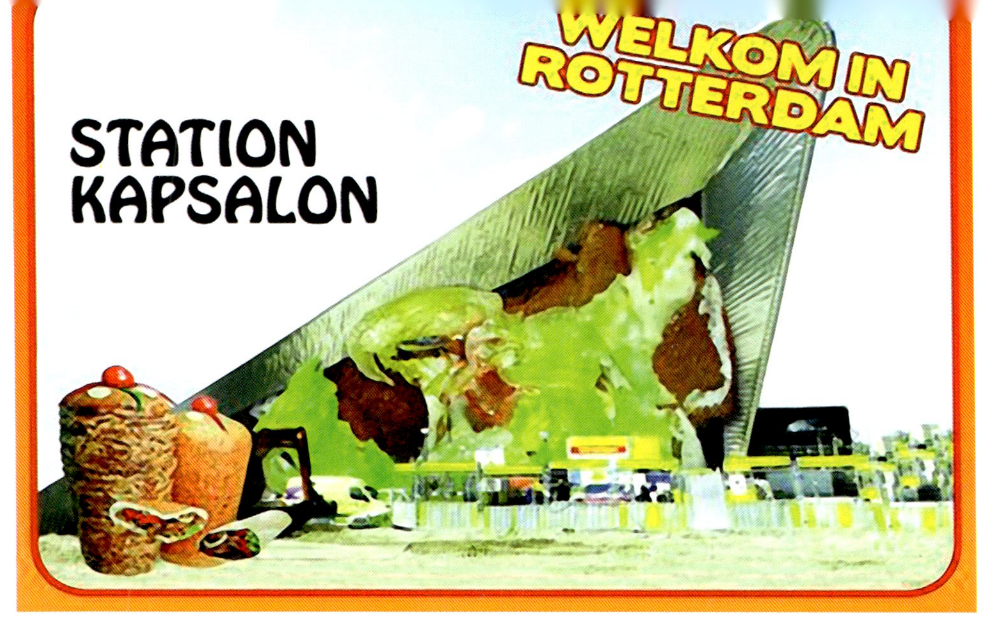
WELKOM IN ROTTERDAM
STATION KAPSALON

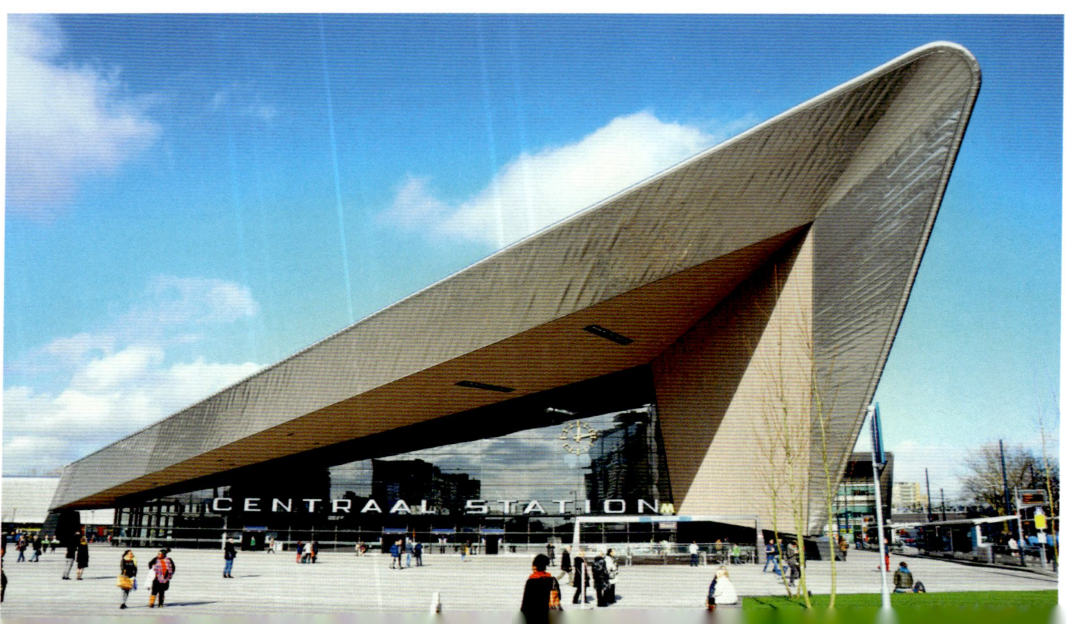
CENTRAAL STATION

Are We Obsidian?

Excerpt of Ellen Gallagher in conversation with Adrienne Edwards at
The Broad Museum, Los Angeles, February 2017

AE: When you talk about characters, [are they] different from
symbols?
EG: Not necessarily. The symbolic for me is about carrying and the
potential to carry – it's like magic. So a character like a jellyfish can be
made up of several different bodies, can exist at different times, can be a
character that's symbolic.
AE: Perhaps you can talk about the Kapsalon paintings, particularly
in the context of working in Rotterdam.
EG: Kapsalon means barbershop, hair salon, in Dutch.
AE: And these paintings were included in the 2015 Istanbul Biennial.
EG: Yes. I was thinking about the erasure of black-being and the
potential of black paintings. These paintings are made with rubber slabs,
they build out, but they also fall in like a petri dish. They become elastic.
          Kapsalon is a dish that was created when a Rotterdam-based
Cape Verdean hairdresser went into a shawarma shop and made a food
collage out of a shawarma dish. Then really got a taste for it – Kapsalon
became his standing lunch order. It's essentially shawarma, fries,
Dutch cheese, lettuce, mayonnaise, sambal sauce, spice, and salad
dressing layered into a segmented tin takeaway container. It's become the
most widely recognized Dutch nouveau cuisine.
          I like the idea of all these ingredients [becoming] fluid in a tin
takeout container. In these divisive times, black and brown men in
Rotterdam have created this relational space together. It is also about
accepting somebody coming in, adopting and transforming your thing and
turning it into something that is now what I consider the Dutch national
dish. In a country that has a very specific ambivalence towards black-being,
this porosity between black and brown bodies within the heart of Rotterdam
is a big part of how I can thrive here.
          Rotterdam was heavily bombed during World War II, it was
decimated. Unlike the city centers of Amsterdam or Paris, Rotterdam is a
working-class port town where the center looks more like Queens than
a European city. There is also this very salty vernacular that comes out of
Rotterdam because it's a sailor town.
          When the new central train station was finally completed,
the people (after public consultation) named it Station Kapsalon. This is a
Rotterdam public tradition, almost like a spontaneous naming competition
of who comes up with the best vernacular for city structures: Station
Kapsalon, de Hoerenloper, Koopgoot … this 3D vernacular is living matter.
          Recently a young [Dutch] Syriëganger[1] was interviewed
by a reporter who asked him, "What do you miss most [about home]?"
His melancholic one-word reply: "Kapsalon."

[1]   A foreign fighter in the Syrian Civil War.

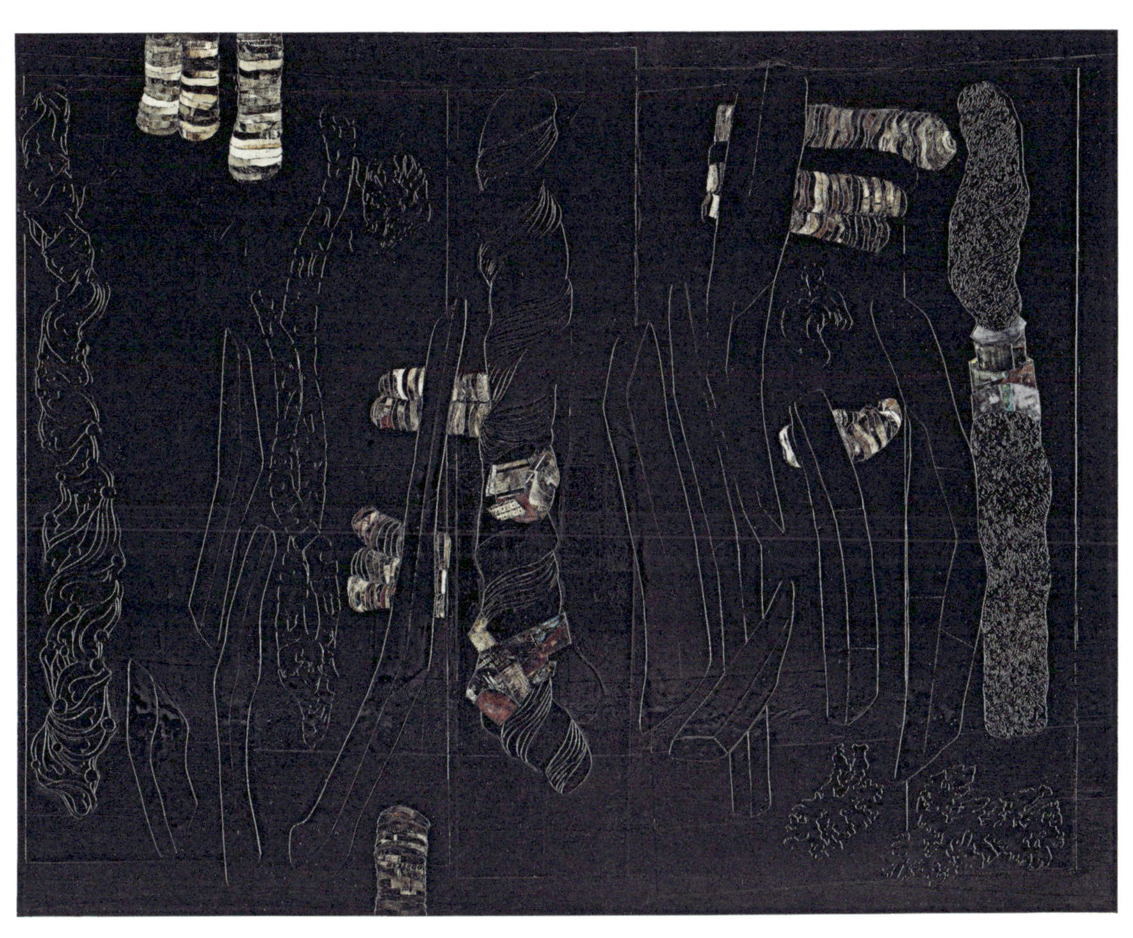

Kapsalon Wonder   2015
Enamel, rubber, ink, and paper on canvas
93 ¾ × 120 ⅞ × 1 ⅝ in   238 × 307 × 4 cm

13

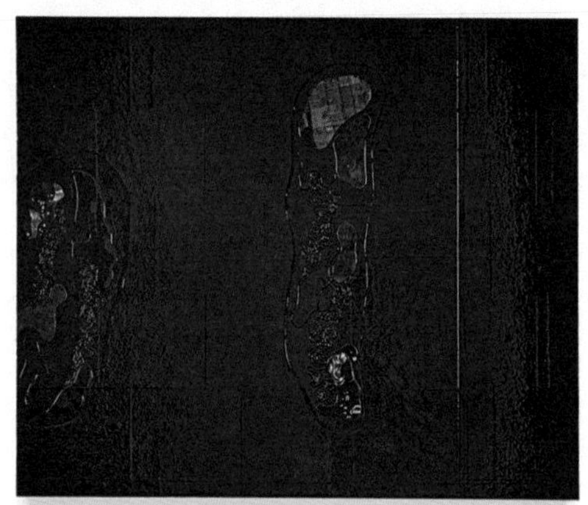 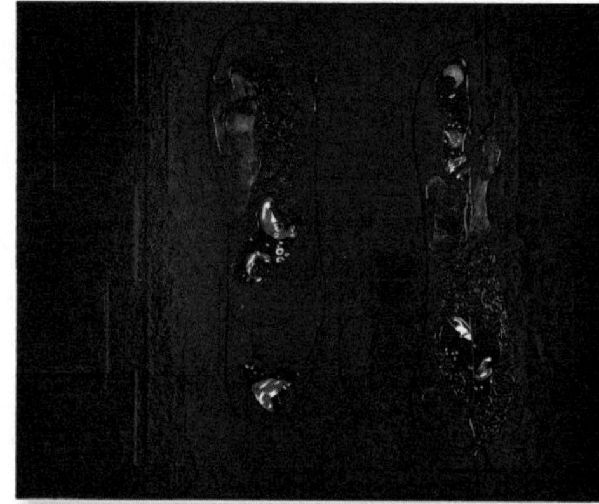

Negroes Battling in a Cave   2016
Enamel, ink, rubber, and paper on linen; suite of 4
Each: 44 ½ × 53 ⅞ in   113 × 137 cm

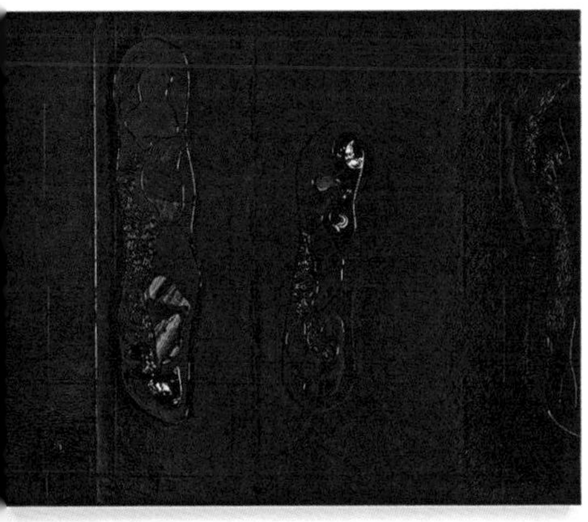 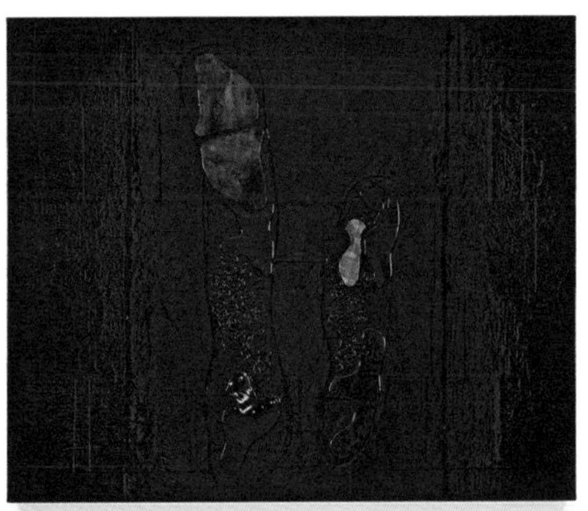

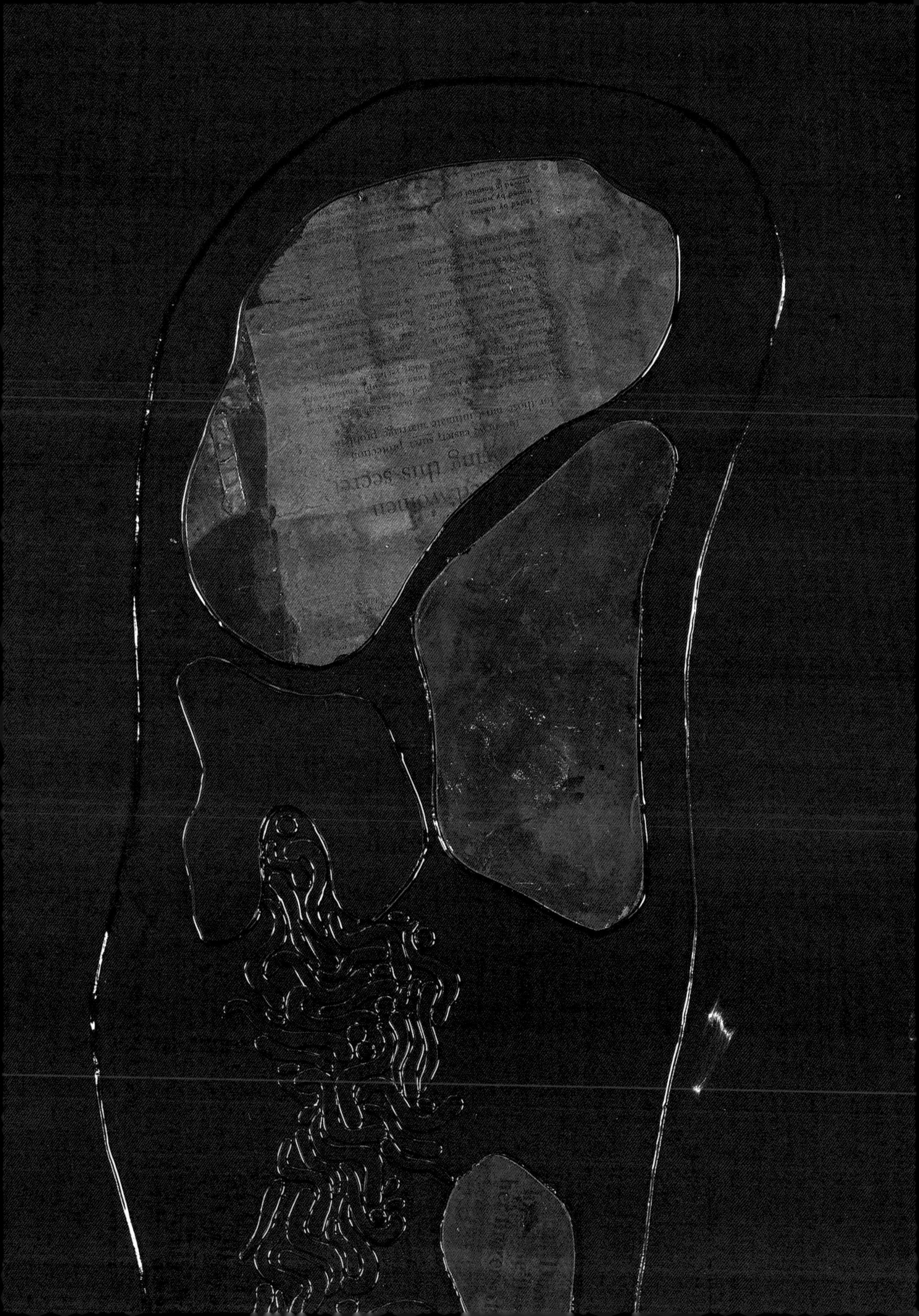

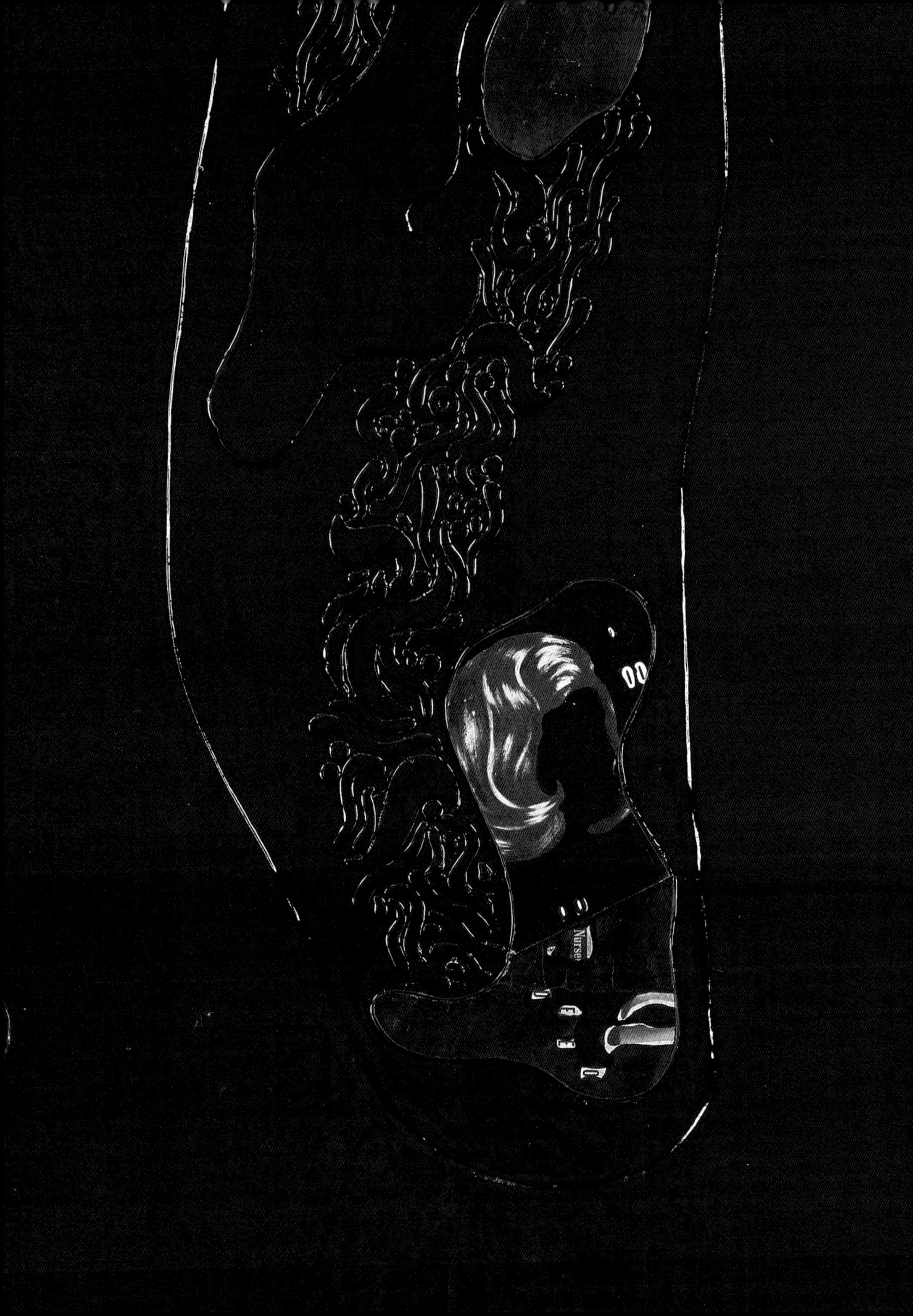

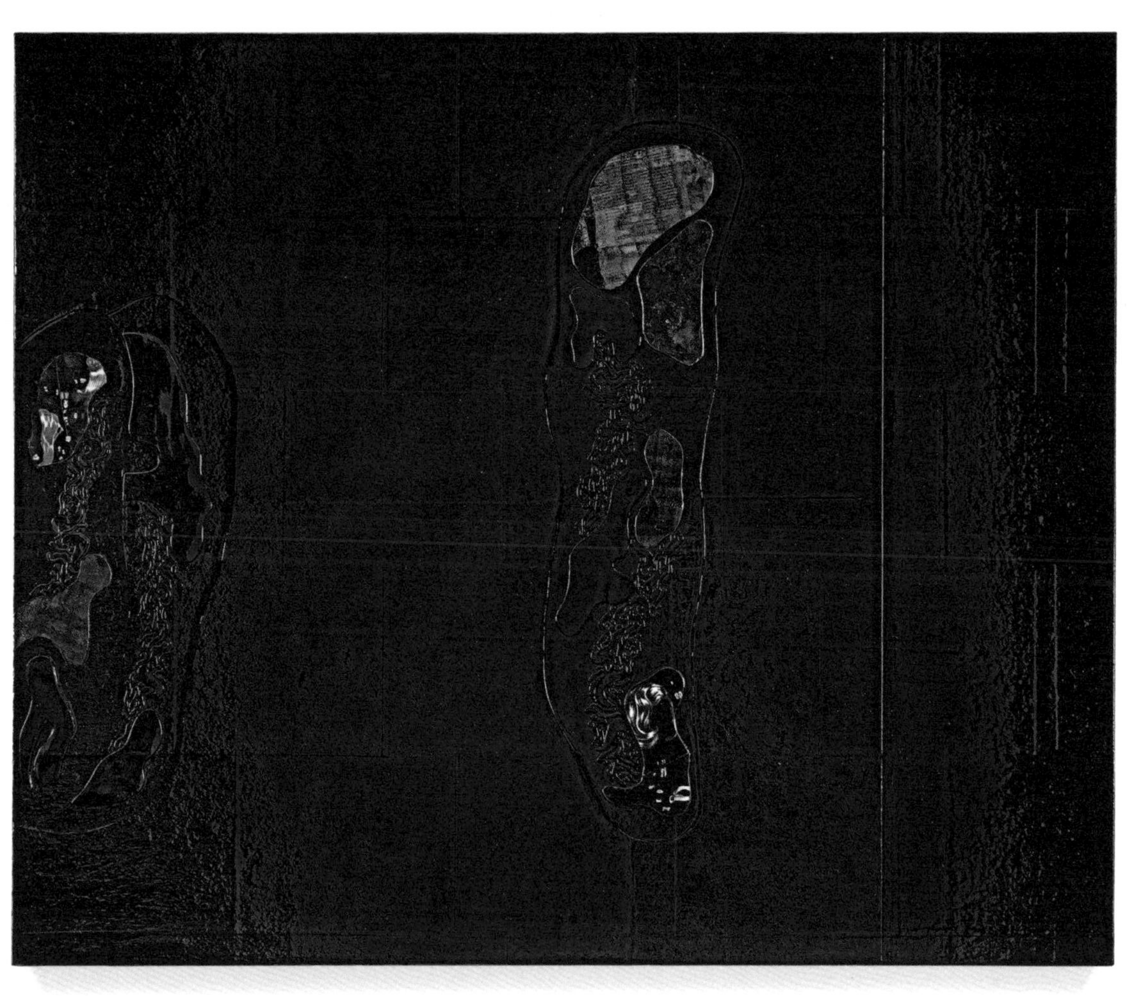

Negroes Battling in a Cave   2016
Enamel, ink, rubber, and paper on linen; far left in suite of 4
44 ½ × 53 ⅞ in   113 × 137 cm

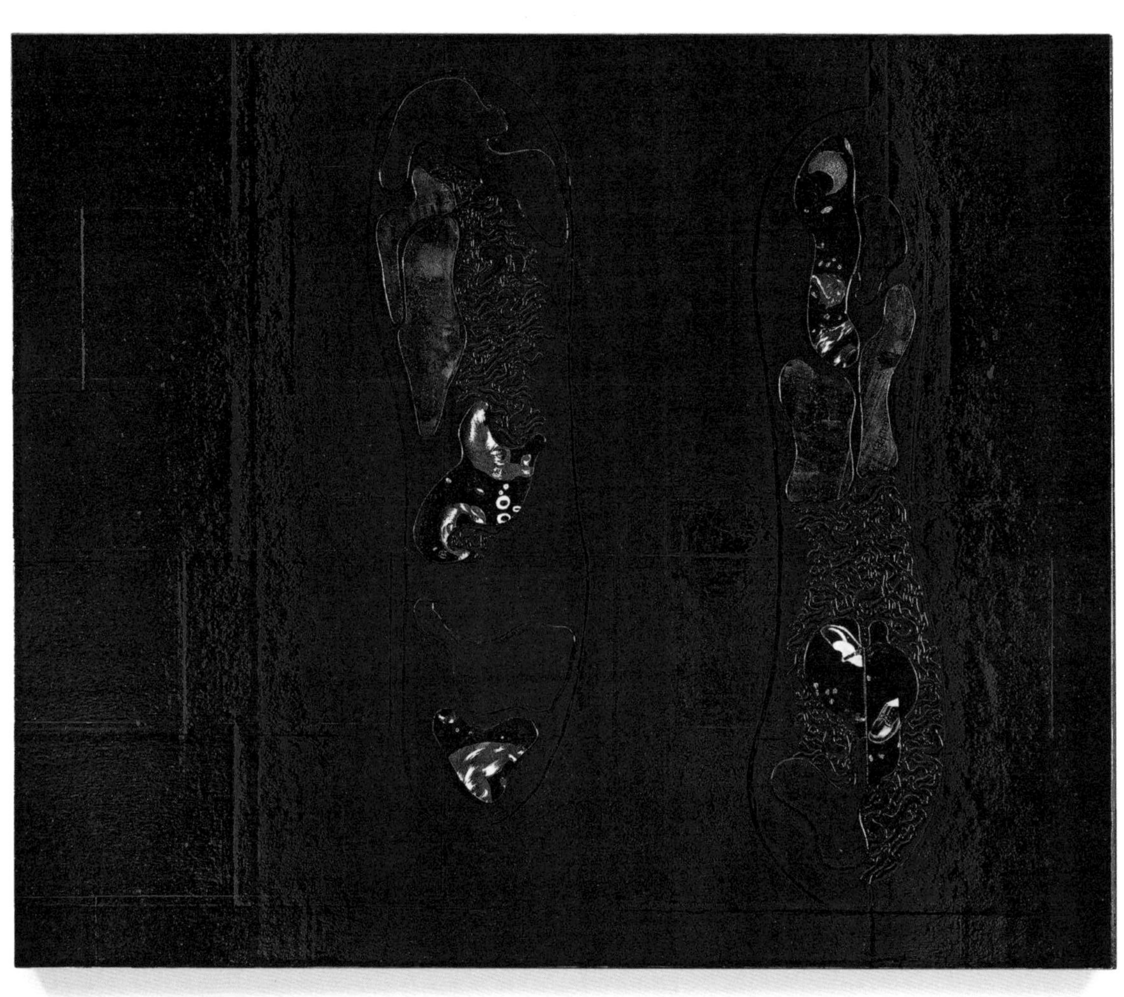

Negroes Battling in a Cave   2016
Enamel, ink, rubber, and paper on linen; second from left in suite of 4
44 ½ × 53 ⅞ in   113 × 137 cm

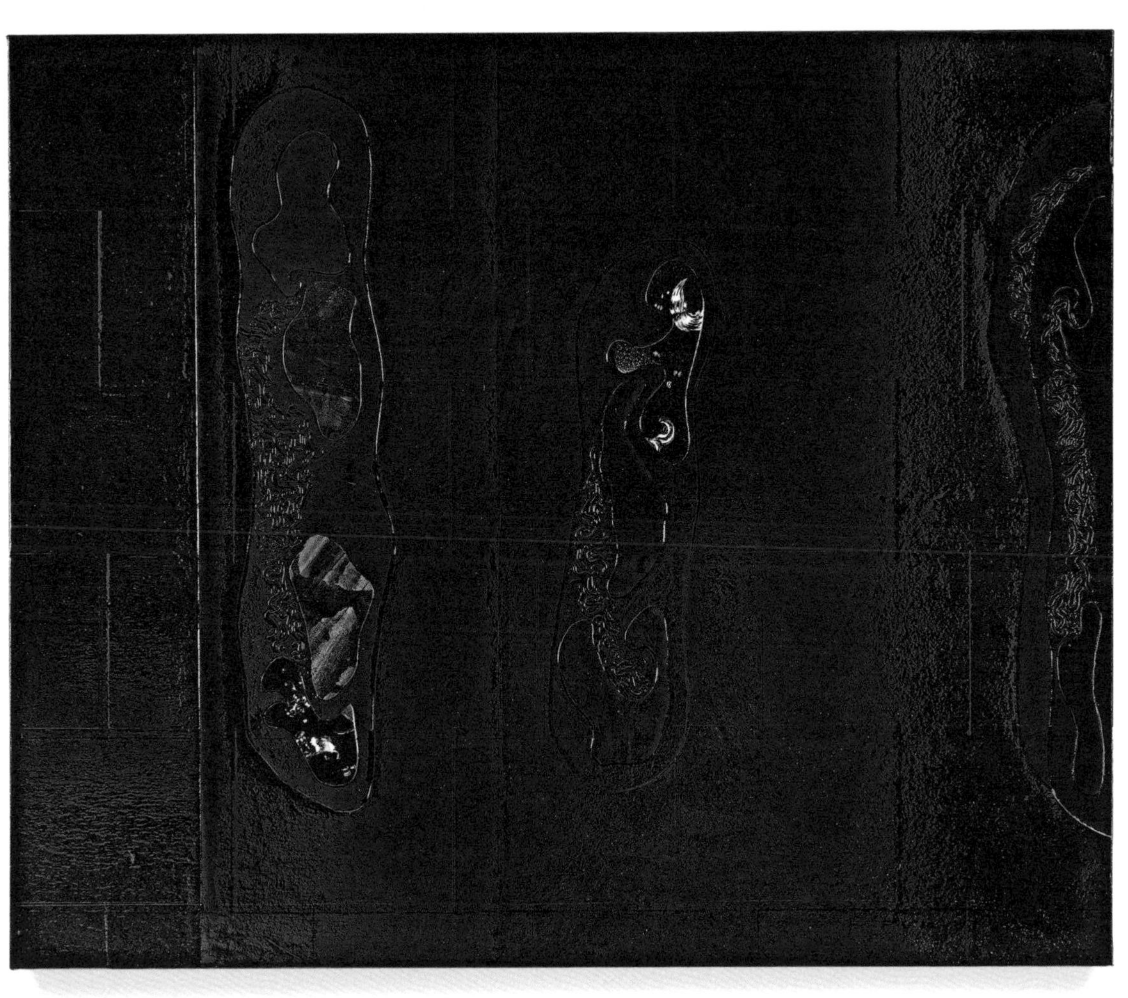

Negroes Battling in a Cave   2016
Enamel, ink, rubber, and paper on linen; second from right in suite of 4
44 ½ × 53 ⅞ in   113 × 137 cm

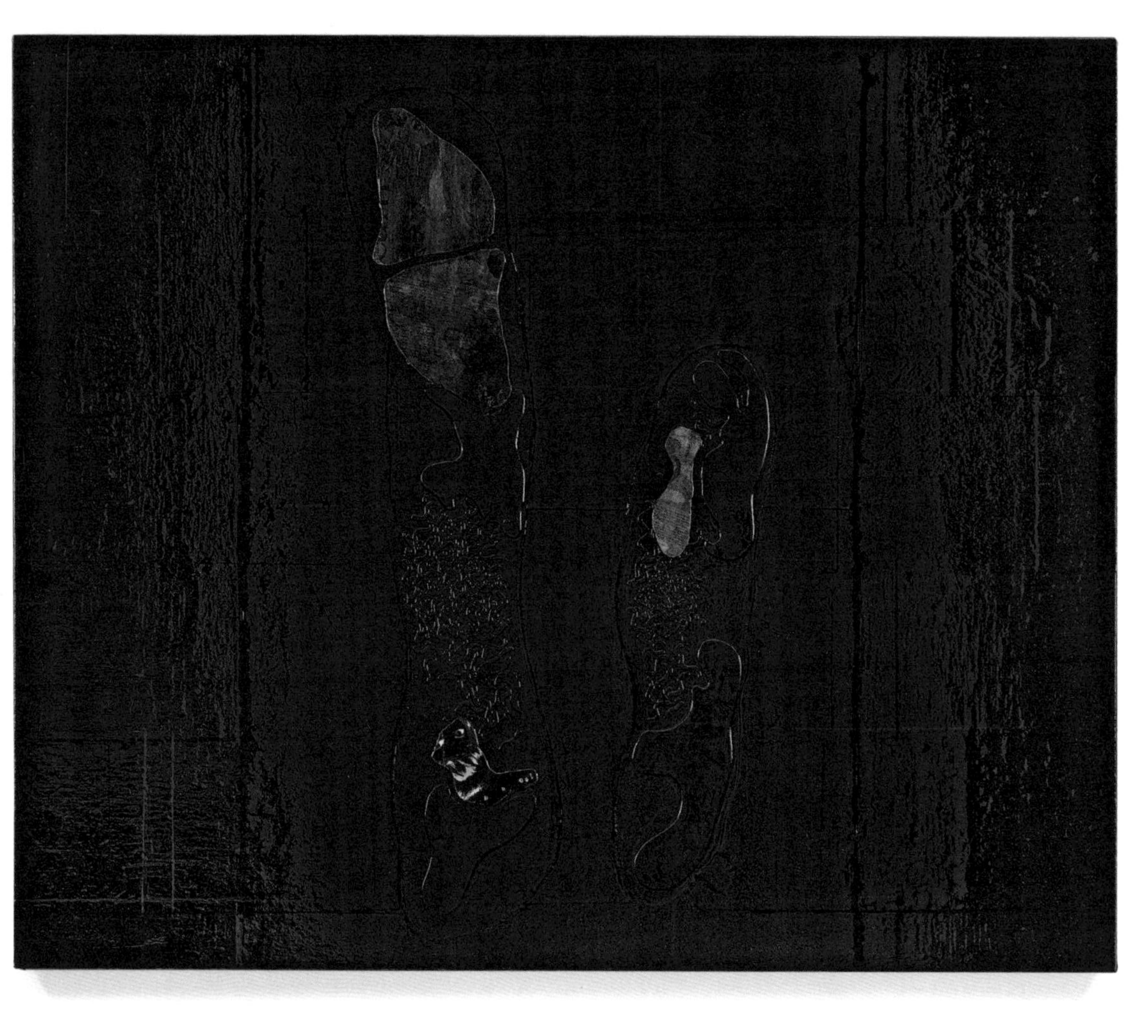

Negroes Battling in a Cave   2016
Enamel, ink, rubber, and paper on linen; far right in suite of 4
44 ½ × 53 ⅞ in   113 × 137 cm

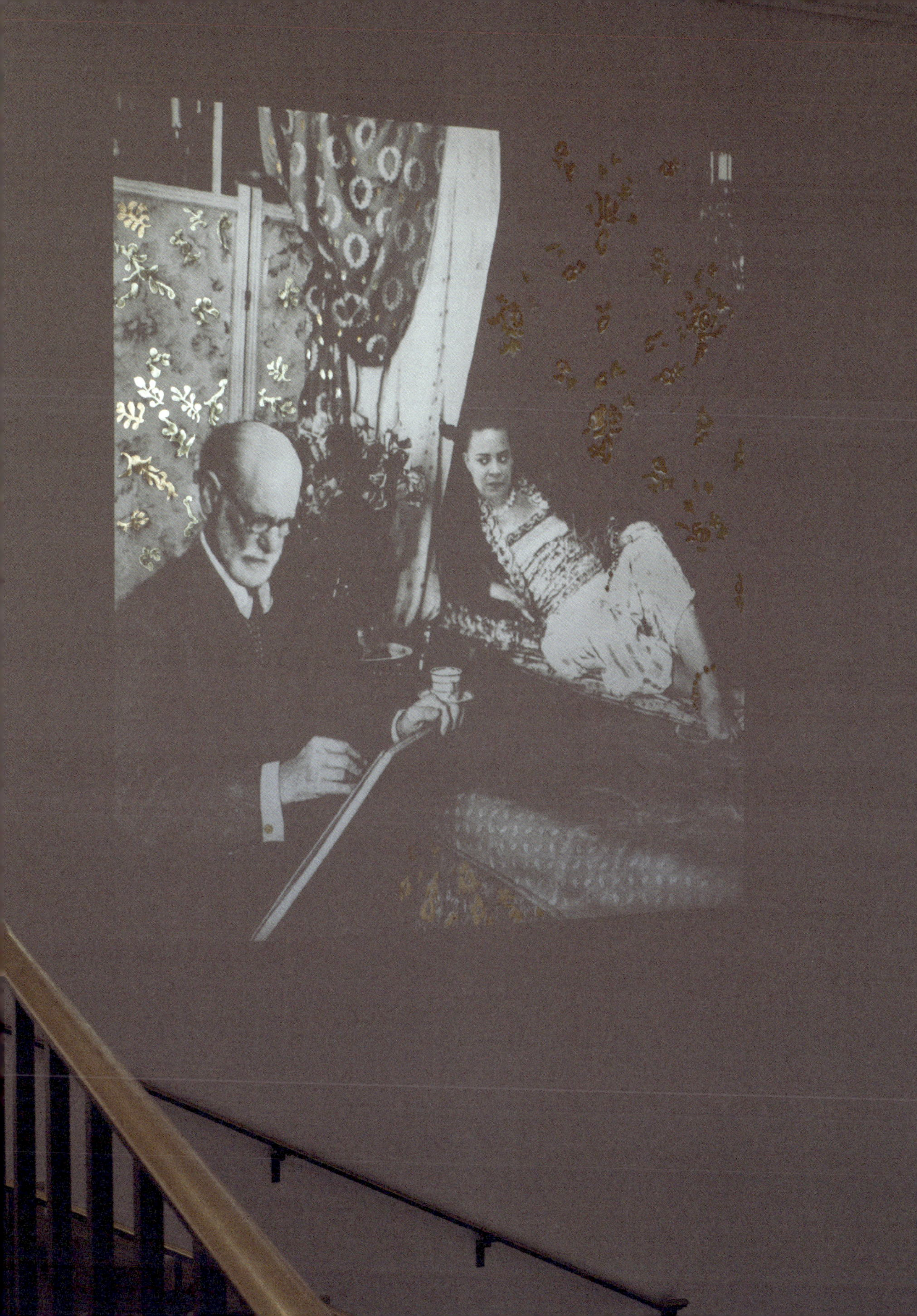

Previous page
Odalisque
Slide projection, penmanship paper, and gold leaf
Dimensions variable
 Installation view: AxMe, Haus der Kunst, Munich, 2014

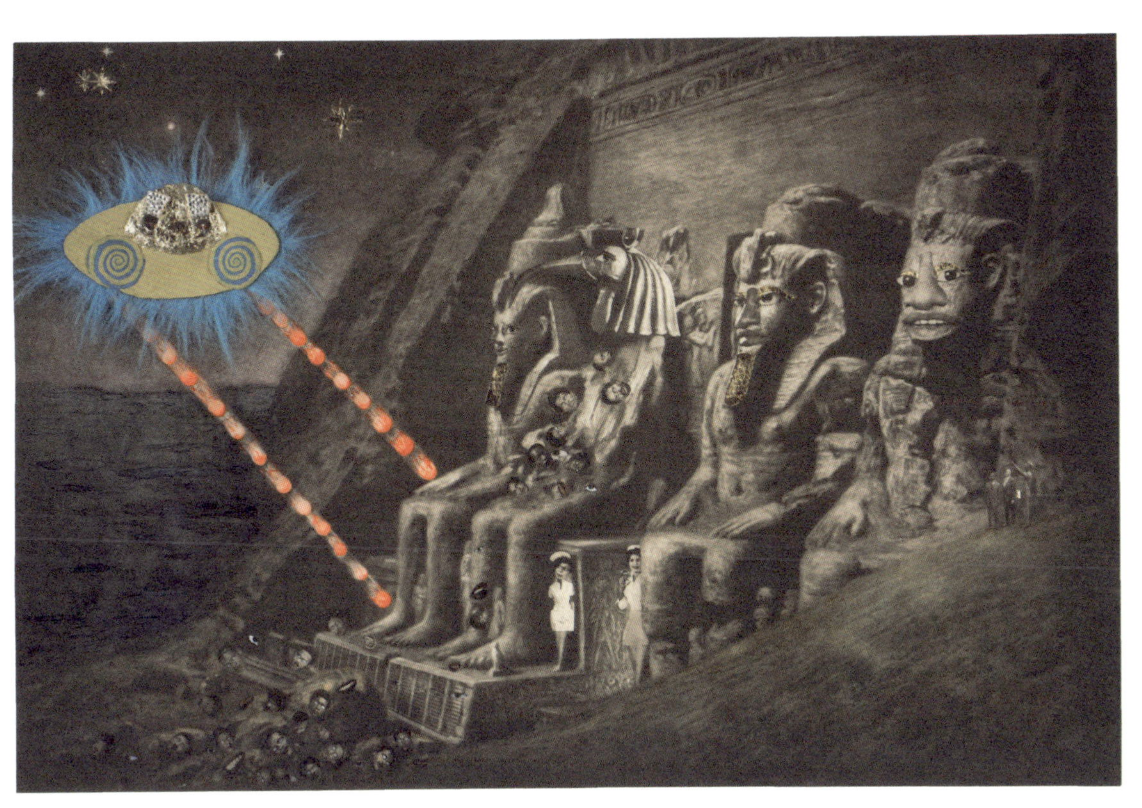

Abu Simbel   2005
Photogravure, watercolour, colour pencil, varnish,
pomade, plasticine, blue fur, gold leaf, and crystals
Edition of 25
24 $^{3}/_{8}$ × 35 $^{3}/_{8}$ in   62 × 90 cm

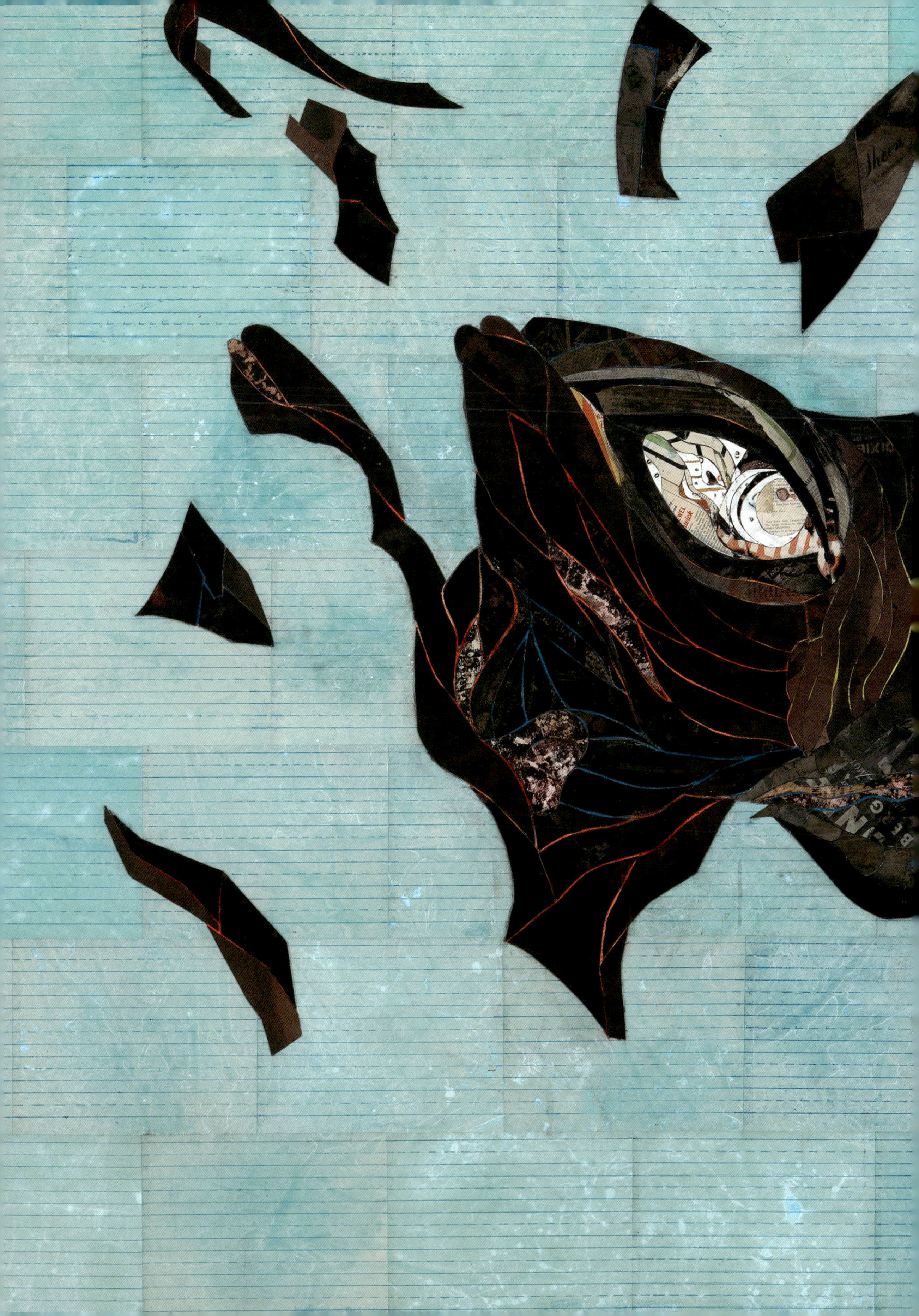

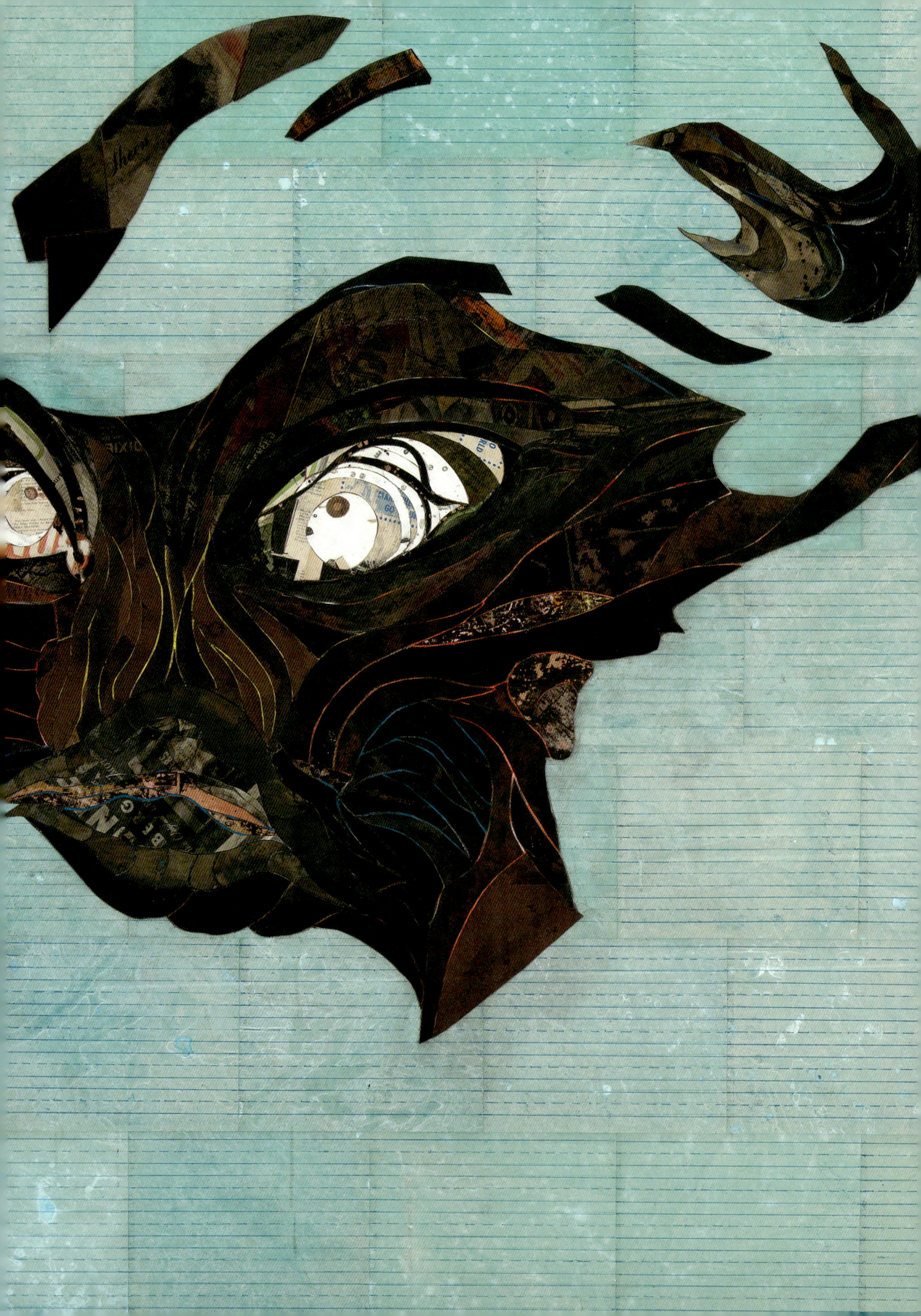

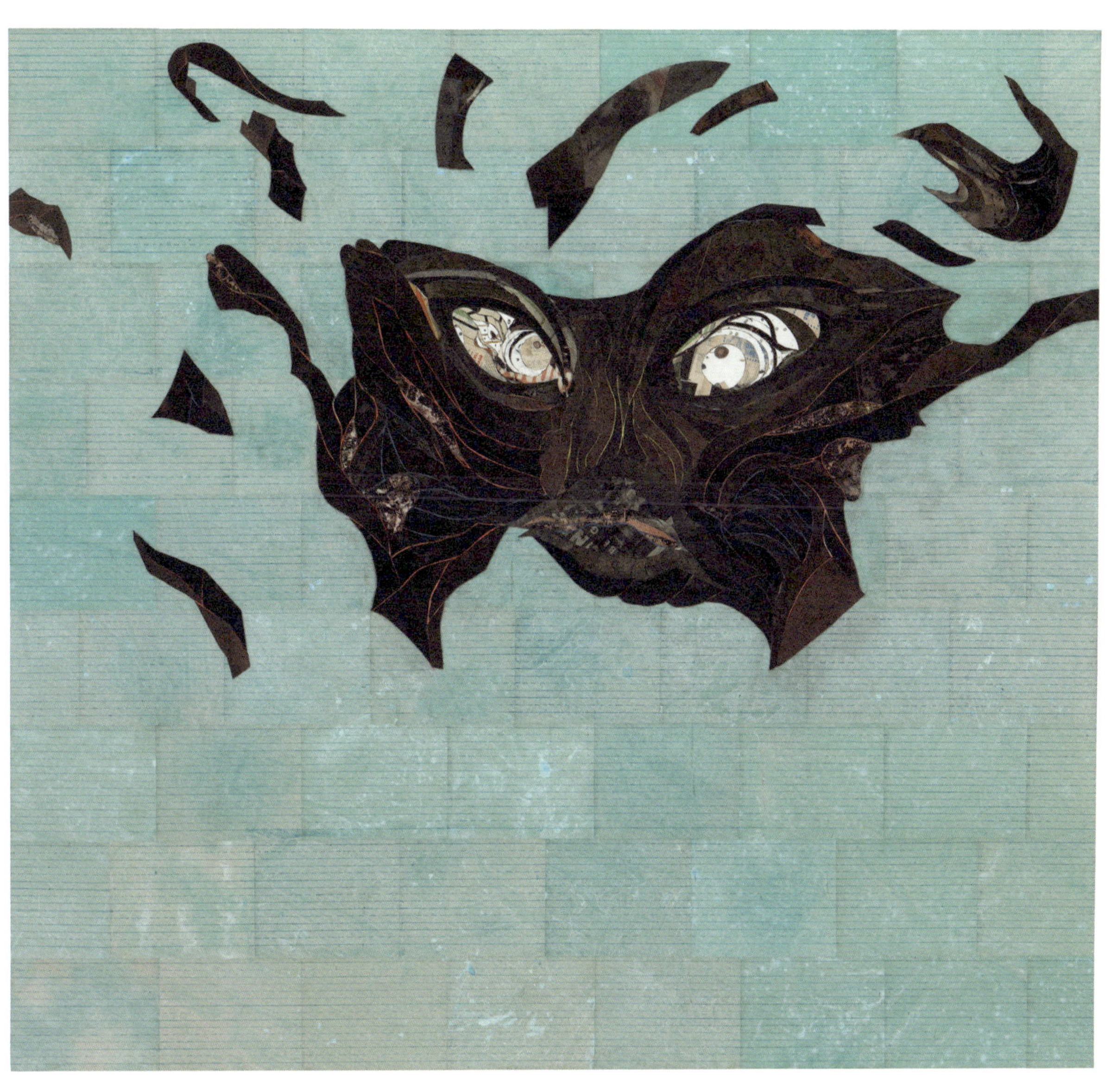

Dr. Blowfins   2014
Ink, graphite, and paper on canvas
74 ⅛ × 79 ⅞ in   188.2 × 202.9 cm
Private Collection
Courtesy Hauser & Wirth

Vectors and Veneers: The Thickness of Blackness
Adrienne Edwards

Whether through her playful photomontages, or glistening veneered black paintings, or chromatic Sea Bed paintings, Ellen Gallagher provides vectors to consider the ways in which abstraction, Orientalist genre painting, and desire converge as portraits of historical, social, and personal imaginaries. Her speculative approach sieves a broad range of seemingly incommensurable references as concrete fragments that we cannot easily trace or fully comprehend, but nevertheless, must. She engages the paradoxes she sets up and upon which she depends through a mode of archaeological extraction of history and matter. In her artworks, Gallagher relies upon what she has described as a "jitter," a mode of becoming in which radical aesthetic possibilities emerge from seismic cracks in the surface of things; connoting unsteady movement, unreliability, impossible alignments, blind spots, and opacity as a means of escape and flight.

In Gallagher's art, representations of people are typically re-appropriated images from her extensive collection of vintage Ebony, Black Digest, and Our World magazines. For Abu Simbel (2005), Gallagher ornaments a collage composed of a photogravure of the Great Temple of Ramses II (which the artist discovered in the library of the Freud Museum in London, where she'd previously had an exhibition) and a film still from Sun Ra's Space is the Place (1974).[1] Gallagher wittily correlates Freud's fascination with Egypt as well as Sun Ra's, who named himself after the Egyptian sun god. She also references Sun Ra's fantasy of himself as a space-age prophet landing on the Egyptian monument (instead of in Oakland, California, as was the case in his film). She builds up the image, embellishing the four colossi, as well as Ra's interstellar machine, with gold leaf, blue fur, plasticine, and crystals, even inserting a Cadillac grille into the scene. She further thickens the collage with disembodied cartoonish lips and heads that cover the foreground. There are also figures of nurses, stationed at the temple's entrance, symbolizing militant care and healing, as well as protective resistance to the kinds of optical violence prevalent in representations of blackness and the tendency for misrecognition that accompanies them.

The temples Gallagher references were originally built on the border of Nubia, which Ramses had conquered as a symbol of his power, and dedicated to Queen Nefertari. In the 1960s, the Egyptian government planned to construct the Aswan High Dam (a symbol of Egyptian modernity), which would have flooded the temples. From 1964–1968, with the assistance of UNESCO, the temples were dismantled and moved 213 feet above and 690 feet to the northwest of their original site. The temples were rebuilt to align with the east, as they had originally been situated, so that twice a year, on 21 February and 21 October (marking Ramses's birthday and coronation), the sun gleams directly into the sanctuary, illuminating the effigies of Ramses and Amun.[2]

Symbols of deconstructions of power and reassembled myths and structures have long been of interest to Gallagher. As a student in 1986, she visited Martinique and was compelled by the radical symbolism of the Schœlcher Library, named after Victor Schœlcher, a French abolitionist who was vocal against the French government's violent taxation of Haiti as reparations following the country's independence.[3] Built in Paris for the World Expo of 1889, it was dismantled and reconstructed in Fort-de-France. Gallagher's interest in sites like the library and Abu Simbel symbolize her conceptual proclivity for dismantling and rebuilding structures – brick by brick so to speak. This is emblematic of the ways in which what may seem to be singular – or unique wholes – are actually complex constructions, the origins of which are never entirely available to us. The only respite from such a reality is the acknowledgment that things are multiple, diverse, and complex, and that wavering, jittering, and oscillating are the only modes of navigation.

Matisse drawing
a model at no. 1,
Place Charles-Felix,
Nice, circa 1927–1928
(Museum of Modern
Art Library)

Henri Matisse
Artist and Model
Reflected in a Mirror,
1937
(The Baltimore
Museum of Art)

Ellen Gallagher
Odalisque, 2005

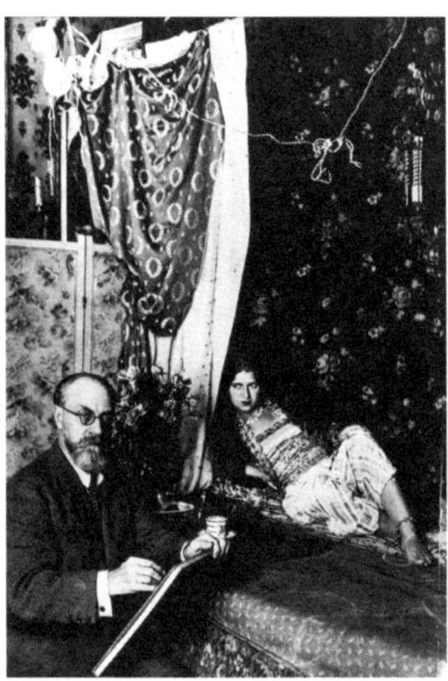
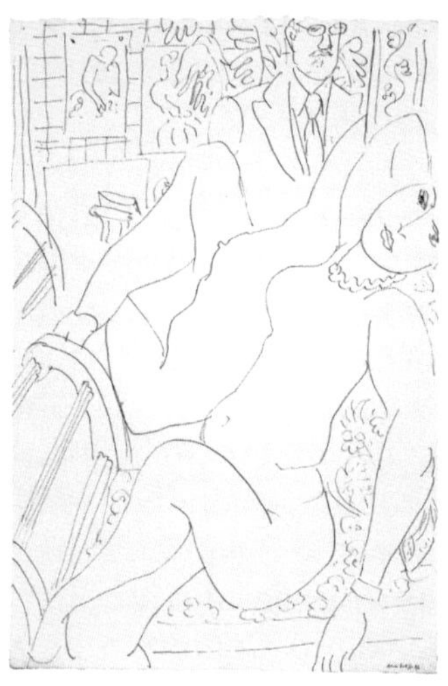

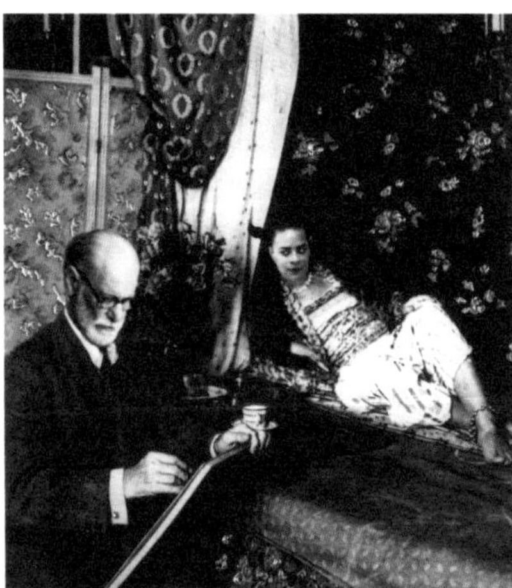

Odalisque (2005), a conceptually similar work to Abu Simbel, is Gallagher's witty take on a circa 1927–1928 photograph of Henri Matisse drawing a reclining model dressed in Orientalist garb, and enveloped in textiles from those regions. Gallagher's image features her own head in place of the model's and replaces Matisse's head with that of Sigmund Freud (the work was created for her show at the Freud Museum). These playful inversions follow a long-standing fascination – if not obsession – with the odalisque as a figure in modern art, from Impressionism to Cubism to Dada to Surrealism and beyond. Orientalist art evolved in the midst of the European imperial project, and consists of representations (often fabricated) of people and scenes in Turkey, the Middle East, and North Africa. Orientalist works are weighted with the patina for a desire for difference. The exotic foundation of these artworks has historically rendered our understanding of and relation to them as fixed binaries. We can better comprehend Gallagher's investment in the idiom when we consider these works as unstable, liminal, and hybrid artistic transformations already poised for intervention. The exotic is constructed inasmuch as Orientalist paintings and photographs are produced themselves.[4]

The figure of the odalisque is one of the most resonant examples of Orientalism's anachronistic and oscillating representations. Indeed, the photograph of Matisse riffs on the French Neo-classical painter Jean-Auguste-Dominique Ingres's imaginings of languorous nude women in Ottoman era harems (he never traveled to Turkey or its empire). Pablo Picasso's Cubist rendition titled The Great Odalisque (after Ingres) (1907), composed of pencil, watercolor, and gouache on paper, is an example of his absorption of another artist's manner into his own. We can trace the burgeoning interest in representations of female concubines in Turkish harems to Picasso's encounter with the juxtaposition of Édouard Manet's Olympia with Ingres's La Grande Odalisque at the Louvre.[5] While Picasso and others in the Paris art world were struck by the radical gesture of the female subject's direct confrontation with the viewer, what is most relevant here has less to do with perspective than with the techniques of formal innovation that ultimately return us to the significance of the gaze and who is looking; a central concern for Gallagher. If Ingres's Odalisque was literally a constructed figure of his imagination, Picasso takes this sensibility to the extreme through acute abstractions that belie distinct physical characteristics of her form. Rather, extending the sense of illusion already in Ingres's work, Picasso reconstructs and reduces the body and the space around it through a succession of sharp, brash, undulating lines. In doing so, Picasso reserves a modicum of the body as line, a sensibility refined through his study and preoccupation with African art as well as the Impressionists who preceded him. The work also rejects naturalism, becoming a primordial manifestation of formal abstraction. Picasso's odalisque's face is rendered to a mere brown smear, a deface-ment Gallagher extends through the insertion of her own image, and counters through the act of dismembering – or more precisely, beheading – the fantasy of a working girl. These simultaneous acts – cutting both ways – reaffirm or even insist upon physical presence. Gallagher makes a claim for the figurative form that Picasso dissolved while also re-enacting a kind of two-way violence – a removal of an imagined woman and the insertion of a real one – realized without the tactility of the artist's hand, but rather through the most representational of all forms, the photograph.

The self-reflexive move of centering the self in these histories is not merely a critique of the valuation of classical themes in art (and therefore modernism); Gallagher illumines the overwhelming presence of desire, the erotic, and the exotic in the ways in which women of color have historically been represented in art. Therefore, in casting herself in the role of odalisque, Gallagher employs a critical framework that amalgamates the history and aesthetic approaches to the female figure by positioning her desire above all others' (even as she occupies the loaded pose of the reclining female figure, questioning this tradition in Western art and thought). Like the function of Abu Simbel, she casts a sublime light into historical and aesthetic blindness.

Gallagher references the role of ethnographic documentary photography and a desire for authenticity as an apparatus of the colonial perspective. Yet, she does so to such an effect that any certainty attributed to these images returns to us as a mirage. The very representations that hold such high esteem in the Western art canon – of which Gallagher is now a part – must be negotiated on the basis of what they are: unreliable, subjective screens for the projection of desire. For Gallagher, the process for making the works, the digital cutting and pasting to create the image, is a slight, aimed to mine and render this history and its gods visually irrelevant, or at least suspect.

The image is experienced as a veneered skein, composed of a tangle of historical, conceptual, and artistic references. Furthermore, the image has a quality of elasticity, as its digital fabrication enables infinite extensions to its web of references. Such are the moves Gallagher must make if she is to complicate and expand the context through which her work is presented, discussed, and understood; which is to say, she aims to negate the effects of misrecognition or the impossibility of being represented. Indeed, for an artist perhaps best known for her strikingly dense and abundantly generous abstractions, it is worth considering why she would decide to make such a pointed critique, a singular outlier in the context of her oeuvre.

I want to suggest that Odalisque functions to put history and our easy overestimation of lineages, artistic genius, and innovation under immense pressure. In this work, Gallagher does not make a proposition, rather, she undermines – inserts a fissure in – what we take as a given. What had been unidirectional, white male desire is not merely subverted, it is taken asunder, stretched like the image itself. Gallagher's pivot on the function of elasticity in the image also illumines the belatedness of Matisse's interest in Orientalism – well out of vogue by the time of the 1927 –1928 portrait – such that this sense of elasticity is not one directional but rather more akin to a constellation of references extending, even mirroring, in multiple directions, enveloping a multitude of power dynamics reifying, masquerading, and exploiting the dynamics of class, gender, and race. In this way, Odalisque is a kind of third rail, an alternative presentation from the perspective of a body and being.

Odalisque brings to mind similar tactics deployed by women artists concerned with the ethics of exotic representation. Rather than inventing, they observe, combine, and portray their figures as portraits of social and historical scenes, as much as the subjects themselves. Art historian Julia Kuehn has noted the varying approaches to Orientalist painting by artists Henriette Browne and Elisabeth Jerichau-Baumann as tacitly different from those of male painters of the period. For her, these women's works have a humanizing effect in representing alternative scenes of harem life, reflecting the artists' focus on domestic themes, communities of women, and portraiture.[6] While these works avoided the clichés of Orientalist genre painting, they still trafficked in a feeling of difference, fascination, and mystery, often replete with the signification of an enslaved black servant.

Elisabeth Jerichau-Baumann
The Odalisque, **undated (19th century)**

Jean-Auguste-Dominique Ingres
The Great Odalisque, **1814 (The Louvre)**

Pablo Picasso
The Great Odalisque (after Ingres), **1907 (Musée National Picasso, Paris)**

Édouard Manet
Olympia, **1863 (Musée d'Orsay)**

Lorraine O'Grady
Body/Ground (The Clearing: or Cortés and La Malinche, Thomas Jefferson and Sally Hemings, N. and Me), **1991**

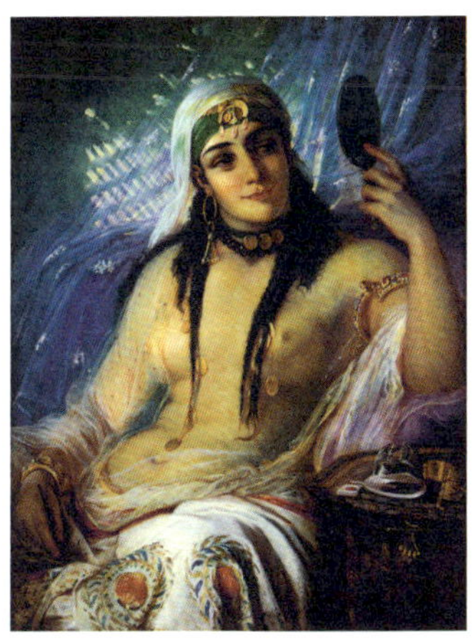

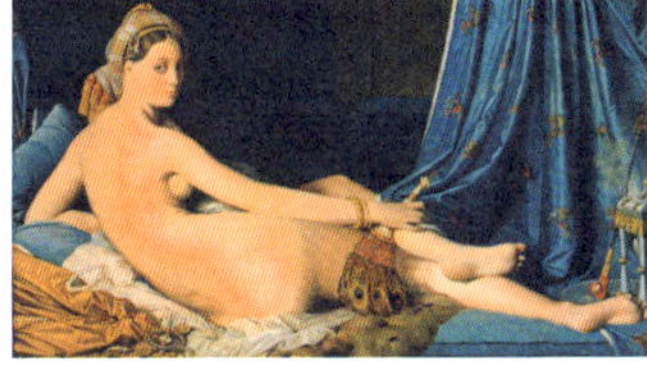

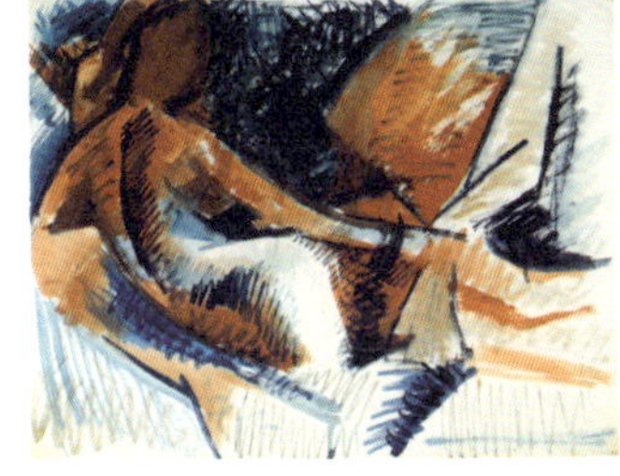

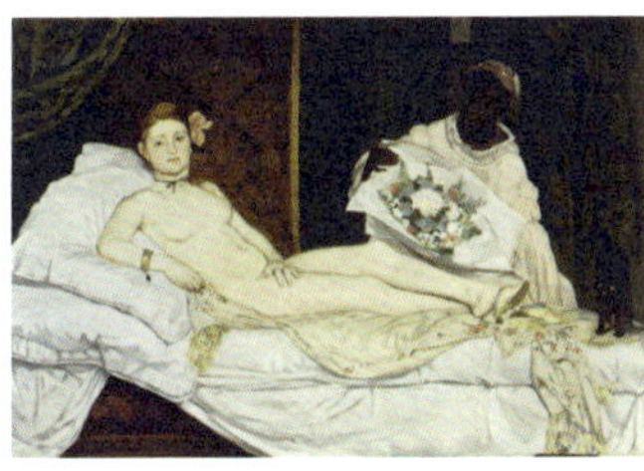

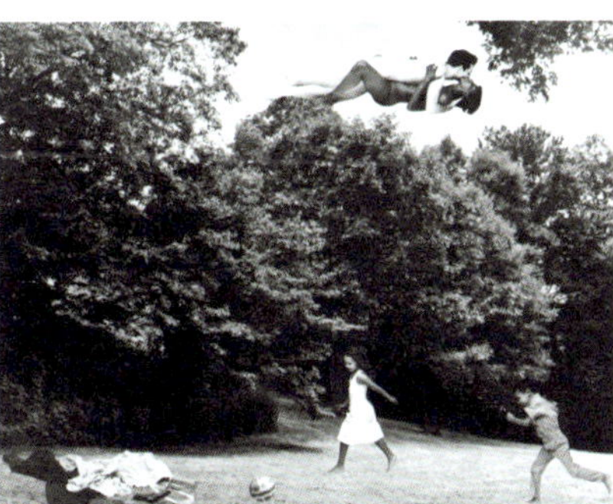

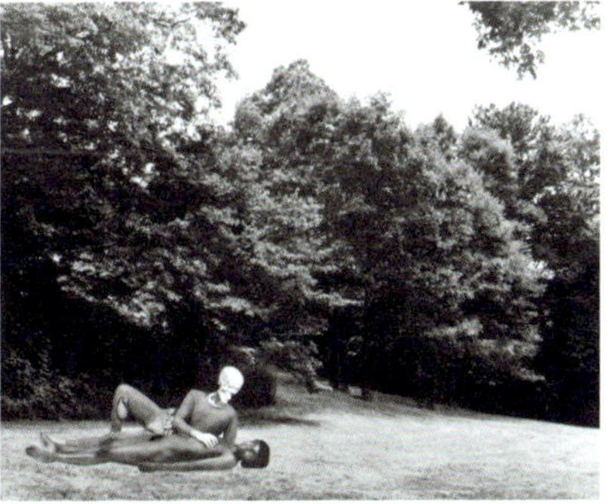

Employing complexity, difference, and desire would not only serve as conceptual currency for women artists of later generations, it would become the very material of their works. We can meaningfully link Gallagher's odalisque intervention to artist Lorraine O'Grady's **photomontage diptych** Body/Ground (The Clearing: or Cortés and La Malinche, Thomas Jefferson and Sally Hemings, N. and Me) **from the** Body is the Ground of My Experience **(1991). Between 1992 and 1994, O'Grady wrote the seminal essay "Olympia's Maid: Reclaiming Black Female Subjectivity," which takes up the matter/**mater **of racial and sexual difference as tools and projections of systems of power that operate to delimit beings through exercising privilege and reinforcing stereotypes and binaries.** The Clearing departs from what O'Grady has described as "the lingering structure of invisibility" by foregrounding the fact of hybridity.[7] Also a photomontage, the work sought to address the instability of history and its relationship to the body and lived experience; the body, particularly the black female body, has been a historical tool for the development of modernity's colonial empires and capitalist expansion. The images materialize – or more precisely, embody – the psychoanalytical critique offered by O'Grady. The presence of Laure, the black maid who looms over the odalisque in Manet's painting and nearly melds into the dark curtains behind her, reinforces the problematic binaries relating to beauty, value, and morality which incessantly circulate in our cultural imaginaries concerning differences between black and white women. In contrast to the tradition of Orientalist painting (and as a through line to Gallagher's portrait), The Clearing **makes difference visible by foregrounding erotic desire and undermining taboos through multiple representations of black and white. Both Gallagher and O'Grady solicit us to reckon with what scholar Robin D.G. Kelley described as a "com[ing] to terms with the racial unconscious, colonialism and its discontents, civilization and its malcontents, the return of the oppressed, desire."[8]**

Unlike Odalisque**, the surfaces of Gallagher's black paintings have been built up to such an extent that they are rendered oblique; the quality of elasticity is distended through the persistent confrontation between the paintings' layers. The canvases waver between their constructed layers – like Abu Simbel and the Schœlcher Library – only to be dismembered as Gallagher draws into them with a scalpel, which serves as a release valve, providing relief from the relentless compression of printed matter, heavy gauge rubber, paint, and manuscript paper. These prescient paintings – thick with material and historical entanglements – are singular examples of the way Gallagher's hand is sublimely resonant in her works, which she has described as "sentient geographies."[9]**

In 2015, Gallagher presented Kapsalon Wonder and Phantasie **(2015) in the 14th Istanbul Biennial, black paintings comprised of open forms, and disembodied braids and clusters of hair. Kapsalon, which means barbershop or hair salon in Dutch, is also a food with a distinctly African and Middle Eastern twist, made of fries, döner or shawarma meat, gouda cheese, sauce, and salad. For Gallagher,** Kapsalon Wonder and Phantasie **is a cultural and historical portrait of Rotterdam, inspired by her desire to make Dutch black paintings or Dutch national paintings.[10] Arriving from**

Suriname, Morocco, Cape Verde, the Antilles, Sri Lanka, and Indonesia, waves of immigrants from former colonies transformed cultural life in this working-class port city. If blackness in abstraction emphasizes blackness as a material, mode, method, and way of being in the world, Kapsalon Wonder and Phantasie explores what black power means to Gallagher as an American, partially of Cape Verdean descent, residing in Rotterdam.

For the exhibition Blackness in Abstraction at Pace Gallery in 2016,[11] Gallagher created a new suite of four black paintings entitled Negroes Battling in a Cave (2016), which took as their point of departure the recent discovery of a racist joke – "Negroes battling in a cave" – handwritten under Kazimir Malevich's Black Square (1915).[12] In this long-lost inscription, Malevich references writer and humorist Alphonse Allais's earlier version of a black painting from 1897 titled Combat de nègres dans une cave, pendant la nuit (Negroes fighting in a cellar, at night).[13] Veiled by Malevich's black square, scientific analysis revealed two hidden paintings – a proto-Suprematist work and a hybrid Cubist-Futurist composition – alongside the handwritten racist joke.[14] These inscriptions trouble our common understanding of Malevich's abstraction as the "zero degree" of painting.

Kazimir Malevich
Black Square (Black Suprematic Square), 1915
(Tretyakov Gallery, Moscow)

Each of Gallagher's paintings begins with a stretched canvas painted in a sienna hue, which is then covered with a loose grid of penmanship paper that runs from top to bottom and left to right. After this, a layer of thick watercolor paper is laid down and Gallagher carves into it, inscribing a variation of the curvy, embryo-like forms that proliferate throughout much of her work, thus making a bas-relief of the canvas. These pseudophallic inscriptions are also reminiscent of batons wielded in fights. In this context, the question of who the "Negroes" are battling is left open (it brings to mind the rebellions by black citizens against state sanctioned violence in the United States, both historically and today). Repetitively interweaving layers of different types of paper and printed material only to enact cuts, carvings, and incised inscriptions, Gallagher gives the paintings a palpable physicality, as random pieces of paper are adhered, inserted into depressions, and cut with razor blades to flatten bubbles. The evolution of these paintings is purposeful, yet open to happenstance, responsive to the possibilities literally close at hand, as one thing leads to another through a process of experimentation and selection of materials. Thus, Gallagher's creativity has an air of randomness, reflecting the importance of chance in the paintings' development. These paintings are layered with imagery from Gallagher's ongoing interest in marine biology, as well as advertisements from *Ebony* magazine. Taking a new approach, Gallagher overlays thick gauge black rubber with this printed matter. For her, it is a difference between forging steel and welding it, feeling the weight through the fleshy suppleness of the rubber underneath the paper. Gallagher then stains and shellacs the ads with shades of black paint, veiling the printed matter in such a way that the images and text come through in revelatory ways. The effect heightens the oscillation between types of cuttings, materials, and colors, as the initial layer of earth tone paint is glimpsed. Finally, Gallagher applies one coat of high gloss black enamel paint, sparkling like the surface of the ocean (a significant motif in her art) to "release the work."[15]

The optics of these paintings are complicated, both on their surface and beneath it, and as a result of Gallagher's archaeological approach, the outer edges are more pronounced, casting shadows through the dynamic oscillation between figure and ground. Taken together, the suite of paintings flow into one another, a conflation of the monochrome, landscape, figure, and text – sliding, folding, coalescing into a sensual whole, well beyond the bounds of any singular form. As Gallagher explains, "In these new paintings, the rubber is thicker and creates a stepped visibility that is about desire and lust. The grid has to do with covering the surface of something that will become more inscribable because it is paper … the weave of the canvas is still visible despite the layering especially after adding the enamel. It is sensual. It is a sense. A working knowledge that is very tactile."[16]

As is evident in *Abu Simbel*, Gallagher has developed an extensive cosmology of signs throughout her career. For her, these signs are "performers" that constantly flow in and among her works. These "performers" are extracted (and thus abstracted) from their original context, such as the ogling wide eyes she frees from the characters held "captive in the electric black of the minstrel stage"[17] that she summons in this work. Gallagher wrests the black body or figure from this troubling history of black performance and its relationship to black visual representation. Robin D.G. Kelley has described Gallagher's abstraction of signs and use of penmanship paper as fugitive acts, and links the subversive sensibility of Gallagher's black paintings to the ways in which Malevich's work of 1915 vibrates and resists matter: "Today, nearly a century later, its surface is riddled with cracks, revealing other layers of color, light and abstract form beneath – undercutting Malevich's claim of having created a work of purity. It is this humiliation that interests Gallagher, effectively inverting Malevich's intentions."[18] Kelley continues: "By evoking blackness as both a color and subjectivity, [Gallagher] disrupts our impulse to locate blackness within a knowable sign – that is a human body. Mobb Deep (1998), a grotesque, cartoonish depiction of four dancing blackface minstrel figures forces us to question why the 'Invented Negro' continues to be a 'knowable sign' of blackness when, in fact, it is an abstraction."[19]

Gallagher's formal technique of layering, inscribing, and cutting a range of matter allows the troubled anachronistic relationship between material, history, society, and culture to be buried and resurfaced like the Alphonse Allais reference in Malevich's work. These fugitive surfaces – hers and Malevich's – are paradigms of resistance, as what may have remained invisible rises through the cracks, animating from within, and up into the raking black light; a line of flight.

The question of what lies beneath concerns all of these works. For Gallagher, painting is a way of manifesting not only the work itself but also the ideas which animate it. She recognizes these lines of thought as historical, social, and political constructs to be unraveled and undermined through movement within these works; both in their relation to each other, and the works of other artists. At first glance, Gallagher's works seem direct and to the point – they have an optical immediacy about them, such as the whimsy of Abu Simbel, anti-Oedipal impulse of Odalisque, and lush seduction of Kapsalon Wonder and Phantasie and Negroes Battling in a Cave. Yet, the longer we take the artworks in, we realize there is a different temporality at play, a slow reveal of all that imbues them, which unfolds as the experience of seeing becomes a jittering trajectory of exchange along craggy, shaky, and slippery veneers.

1	Robin D.G. Kelley, "Confounding Myths," in Ellen Gallagher: AxMe, exh. cat. (London: Tate Gallery, 2013), 19.

2	See https://www.ancient.eu/Abu_Simbel/. Accessed: September 22, 2017.

3	Author in conversation with Ellen Gallagher at The Broad Museum on February 24, 2017 as part of its partnership with USC's Roski School of Art and Design.

4	This argument draws upon Julia Kuehn's formulation of the exotic in Orientalist art. See "Exotic Harem Paintings: Gender, Documentation, and Imagination" in Frontiers: A Journal of Women Studies, Vol. 32, No. 2 (2011).

5	Susan Grace Galassi, "Picasso's 'Odalisque'" in Notes in the History of Art, Vol. 11, No. 3/4 (Spring/Summer 1992), 34.

6	Julia Kuehn, "Exotic Harem Paintings: Gender, Documentation, and Imagination" in Frontiers: A Journal of Women Studies, Vol. 32, No. 2 (2011), 40.

7	See Lorraine O'Grady, "Olympia's Maid: Reclaiming Black Female Subjectivity" http://lorraineogrady.com/wp-content/uploads/2015/11/Lorraine-OGrady_Olympias-Maid-Reclaiming-Black-Female-Subjectivity1.pdf. Accessed: September 15, 2017

8	Kelley, 9.

9	Ellen Gallagher, interview with the author, Rotterdam, the Netherlands, March 13, 2016.

10	Author in conversation with Ellen Gallagher at The Broad Museum on February 24, 2017 as part of its partnership with USC's Roski School of Art and Design.

11	See Adrienne Edwards, Blackness in Abstraction (New York: Pace Gallery, 2016).

12	"Russia discovers two secret paintings under avant-garde masterpiece," http://www.theguardian.com/world/2015/nov/13/russia-malevich-black-square-hidden-paintings. Accessed: May 1, 2016.

13	Ibid.

14	Ibid.

15	Ellen Gallagher, interview with the author, Rotterdam, the Netherlands, March 13, 2016.

16	Ibid.

17	Ellen Gallagher quoted in Suzanne P. Hudson, "1000 Words: Ellen Gallagher" in Artforum, April 2004.

18	Kelley, 11.

19	Ibid.

*   *   *

Adrienne Edwards is curator at large, Walker Art Center and curator, Performa.

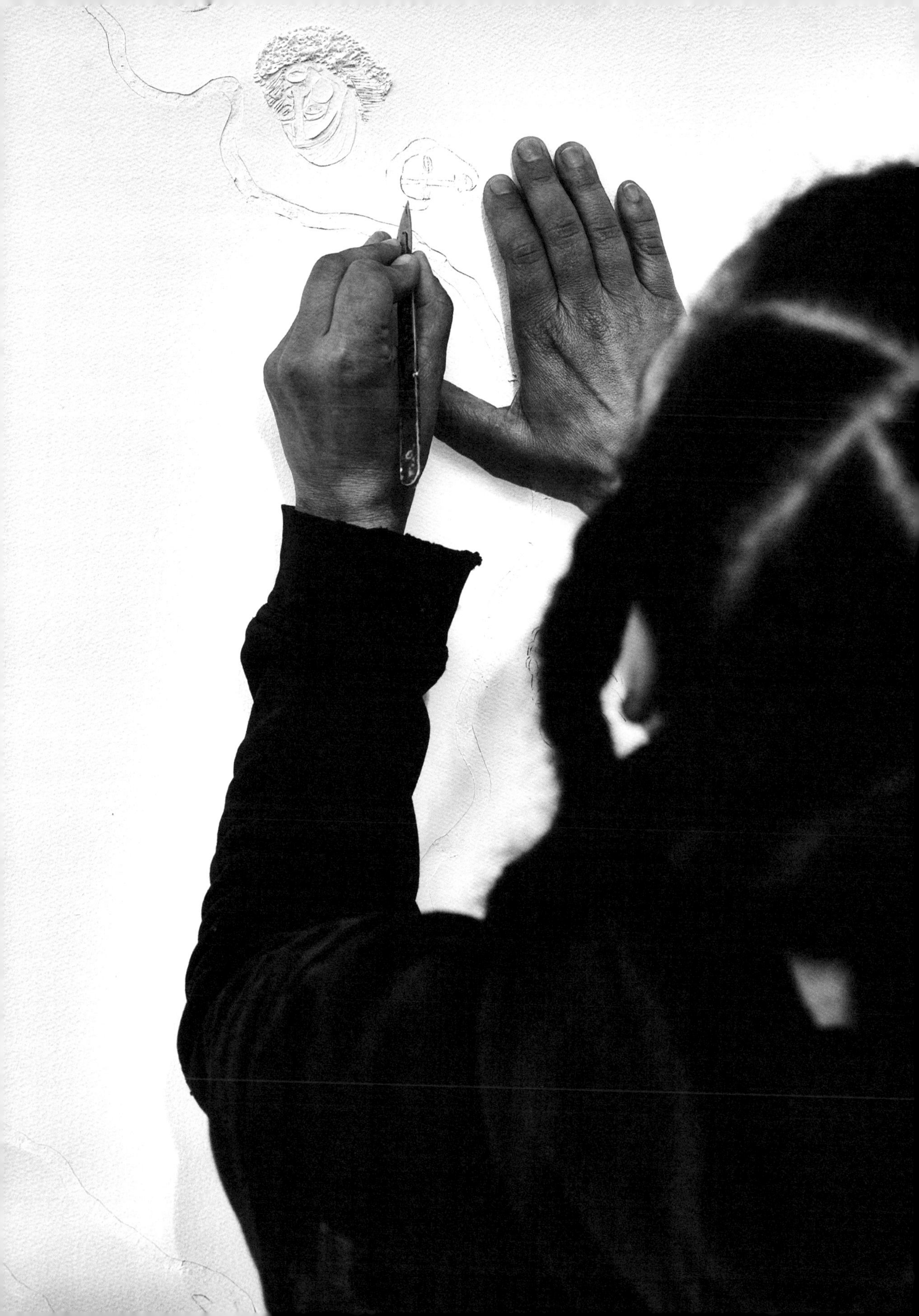

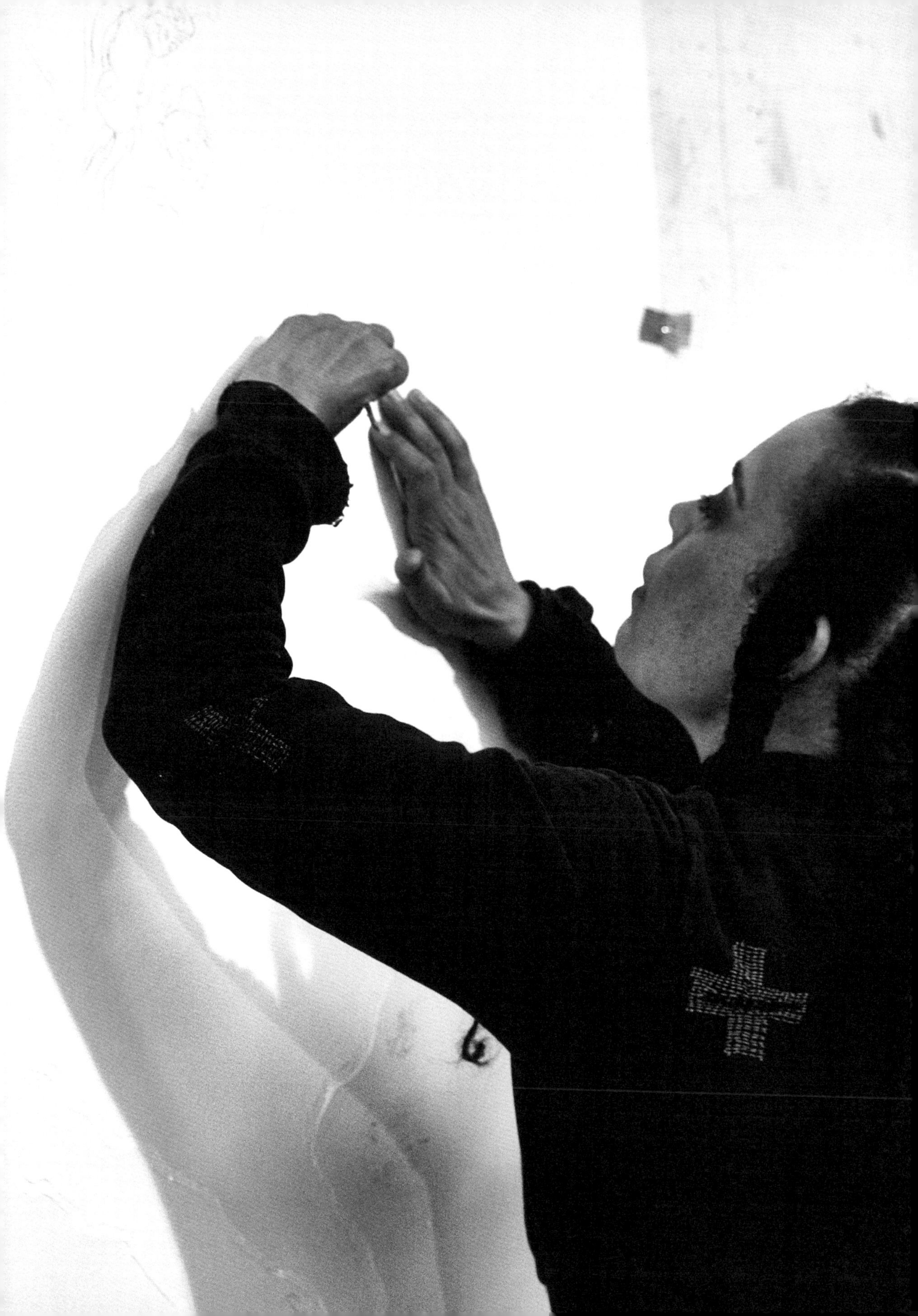

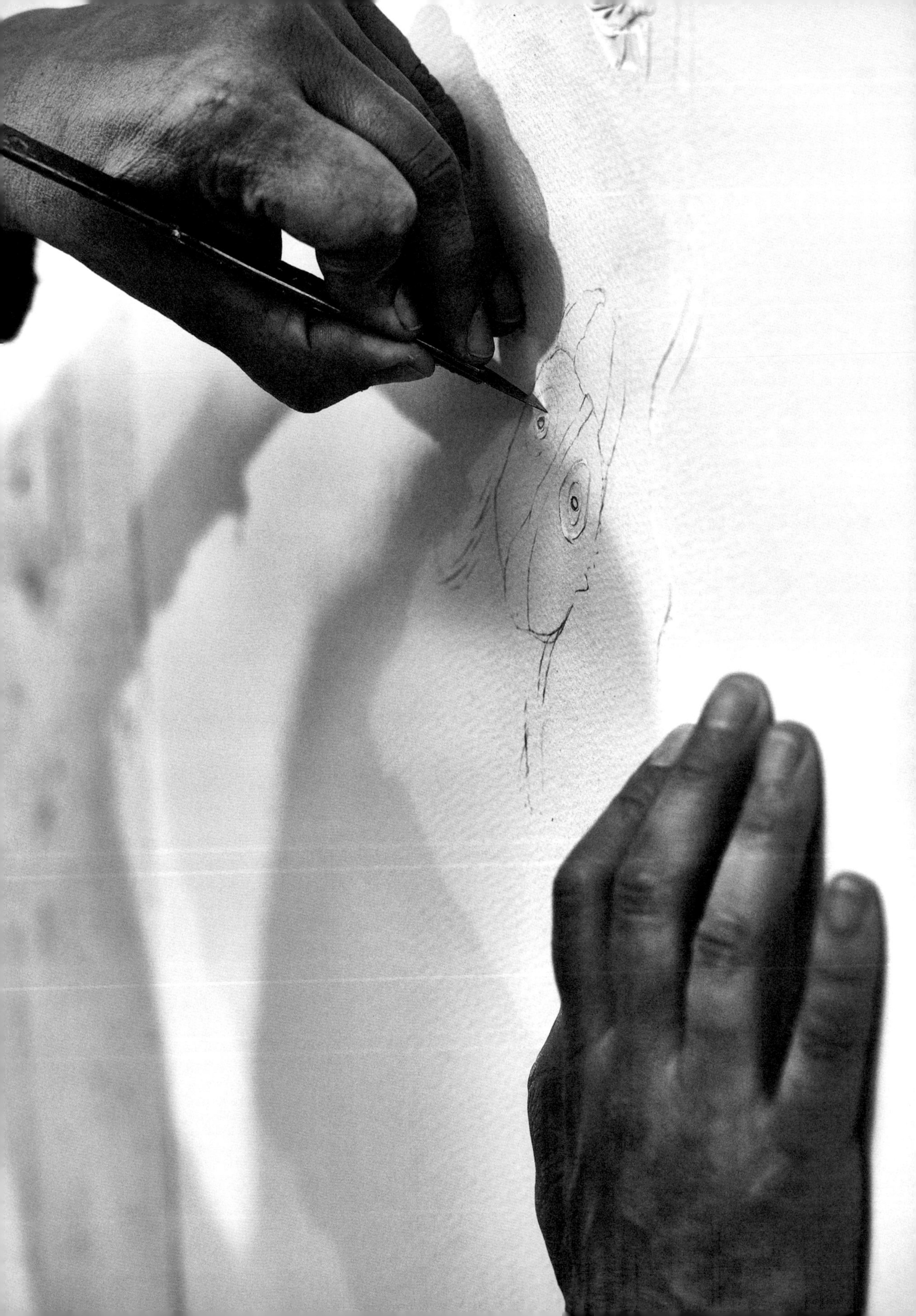

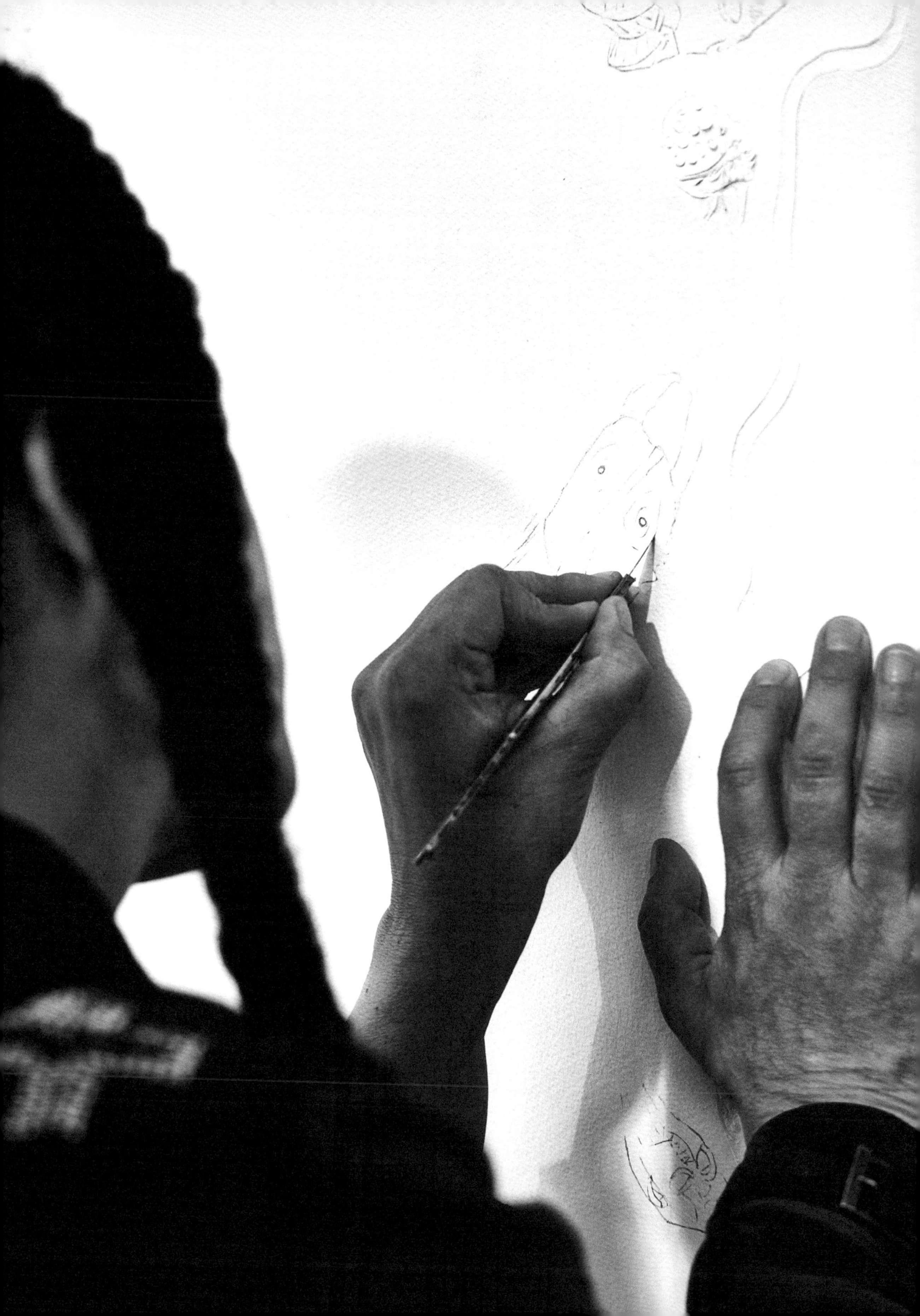

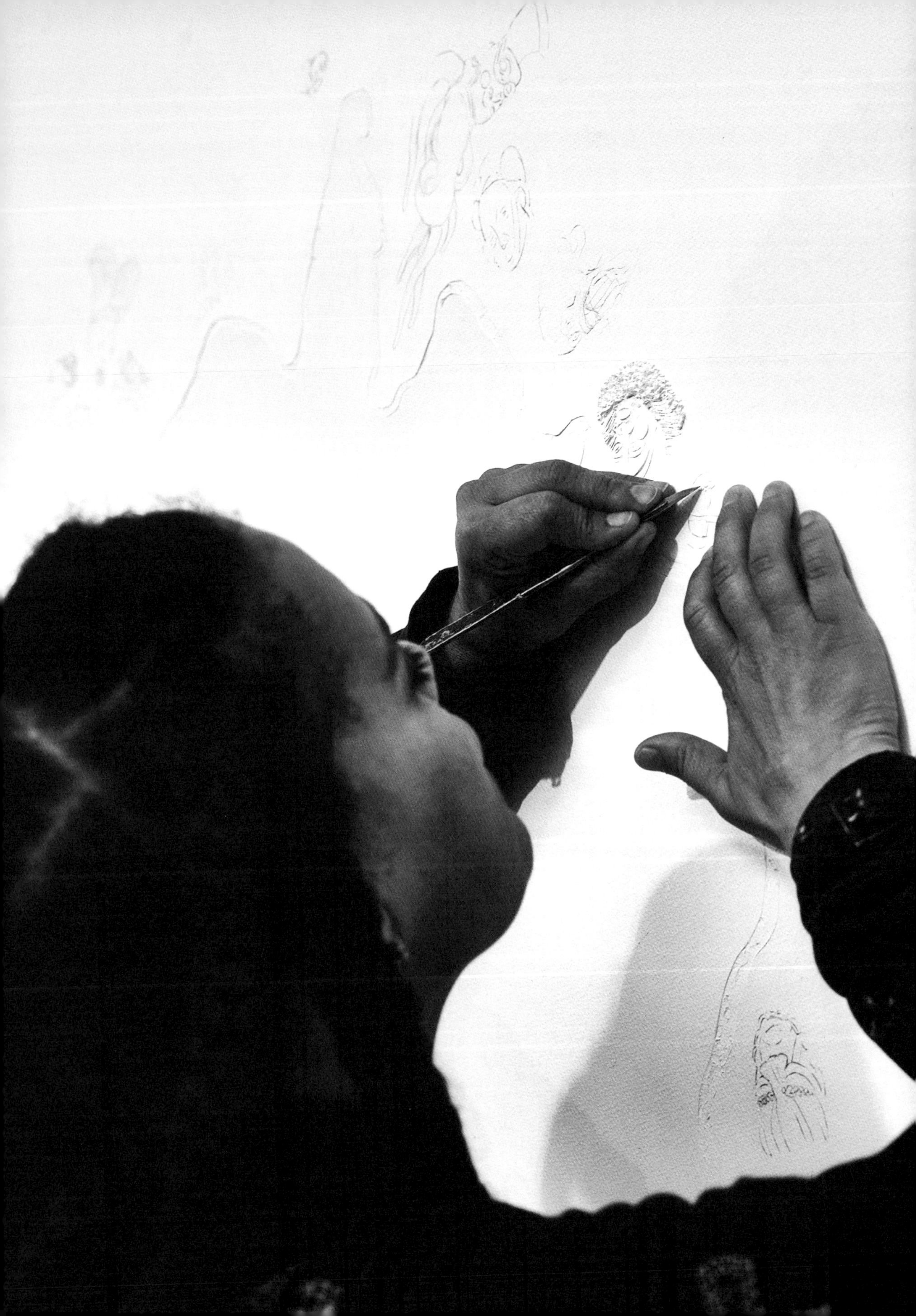

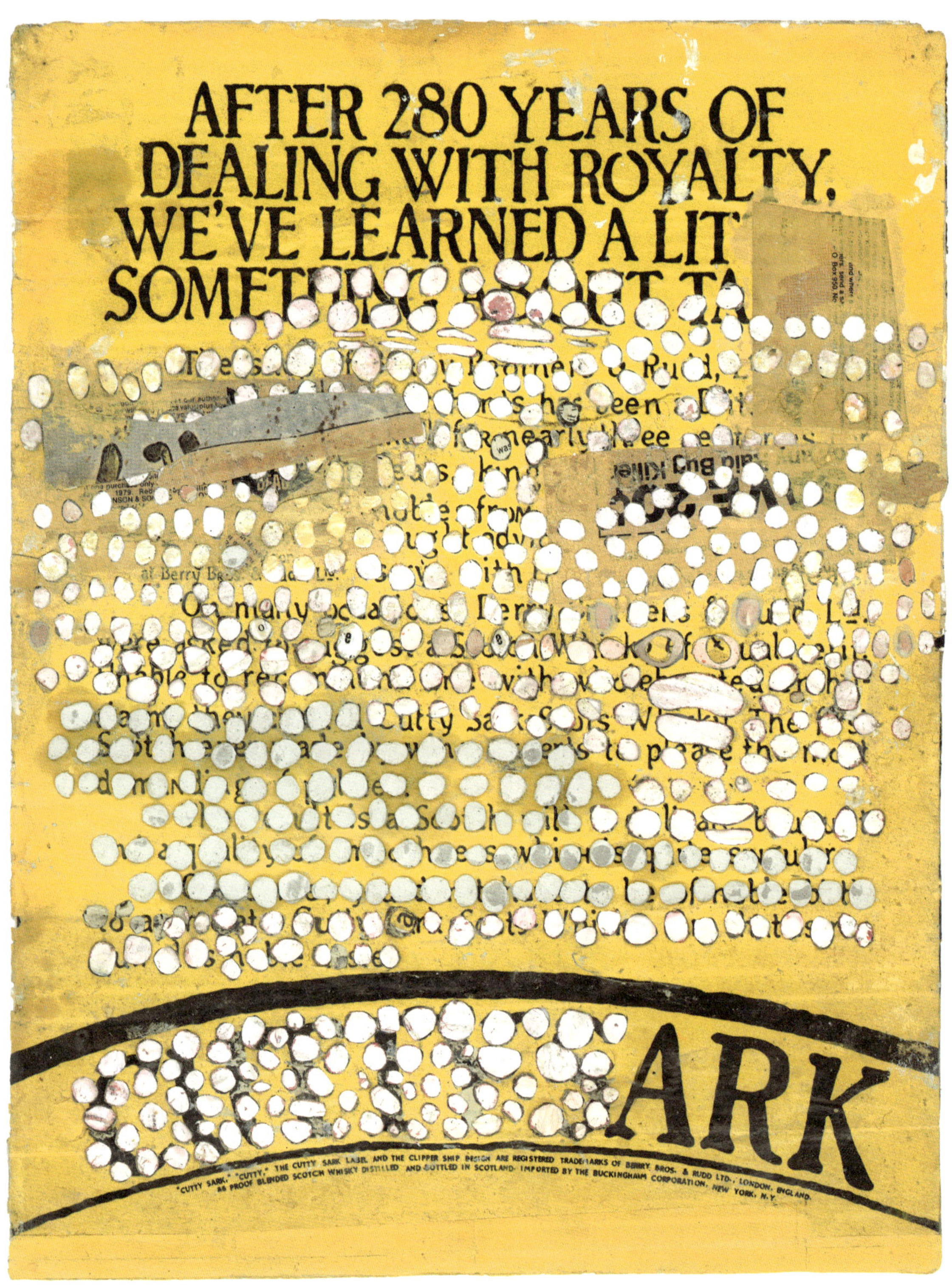

Ark   2014
Gouache and plasticine on cut paper
Two-sided work on paper

50   13 ⅛ × 10 ⅛ in   33.3 × 25.6 cm

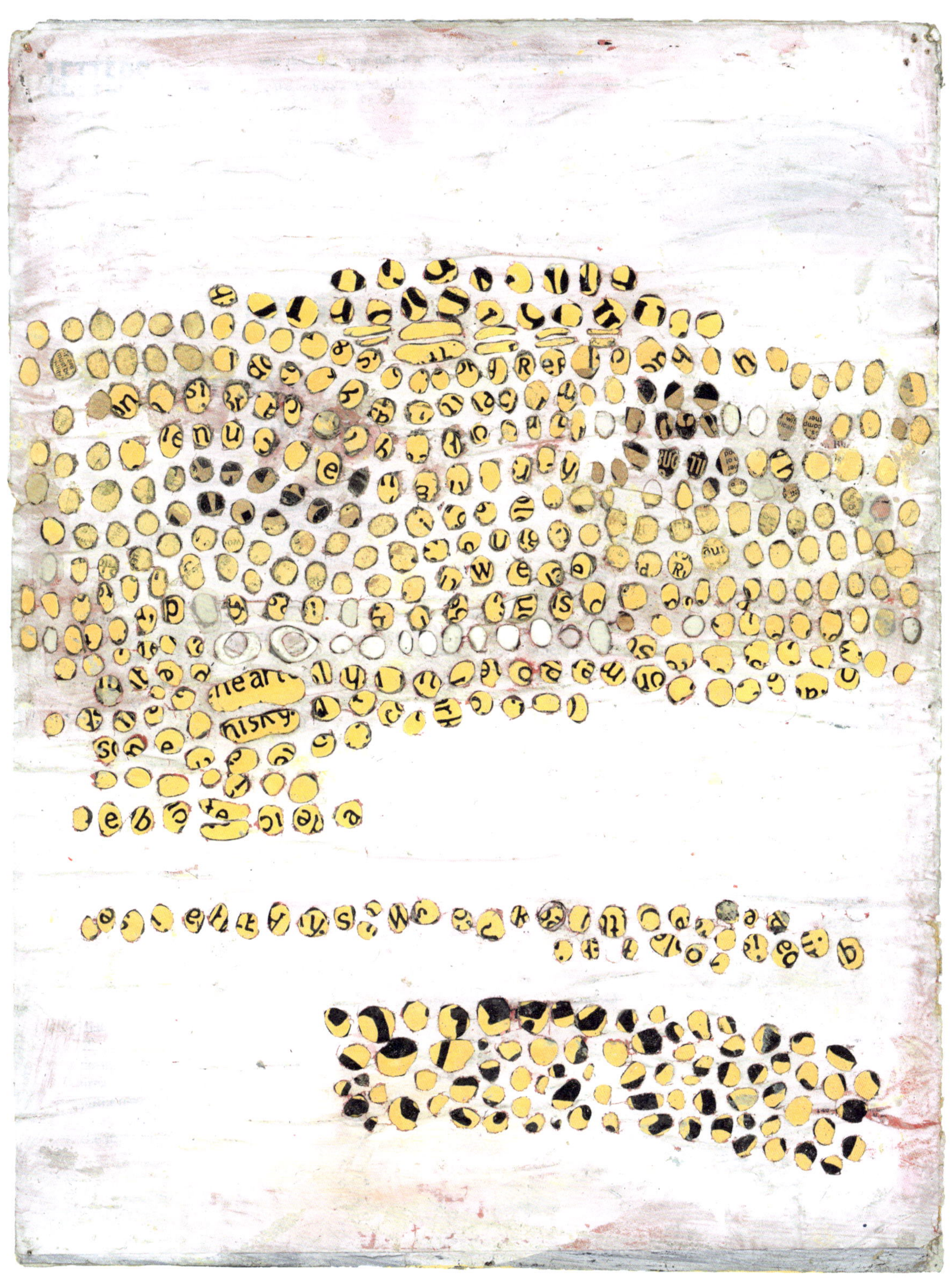

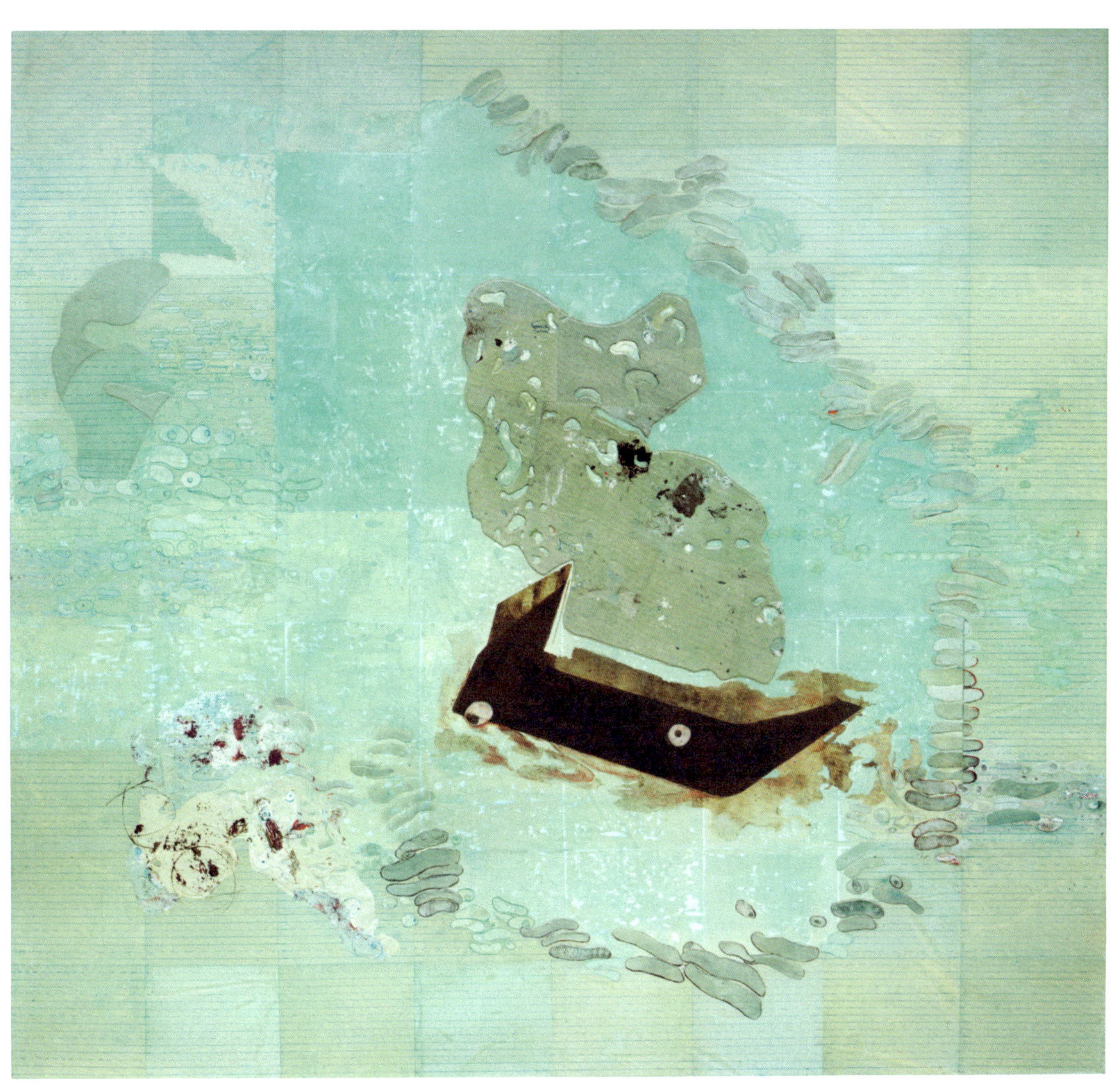

Whale Fall   2017
Oil, acrylic, ink, and paper on canvas
74 × 79 ½ in   188 × 202 cm

53

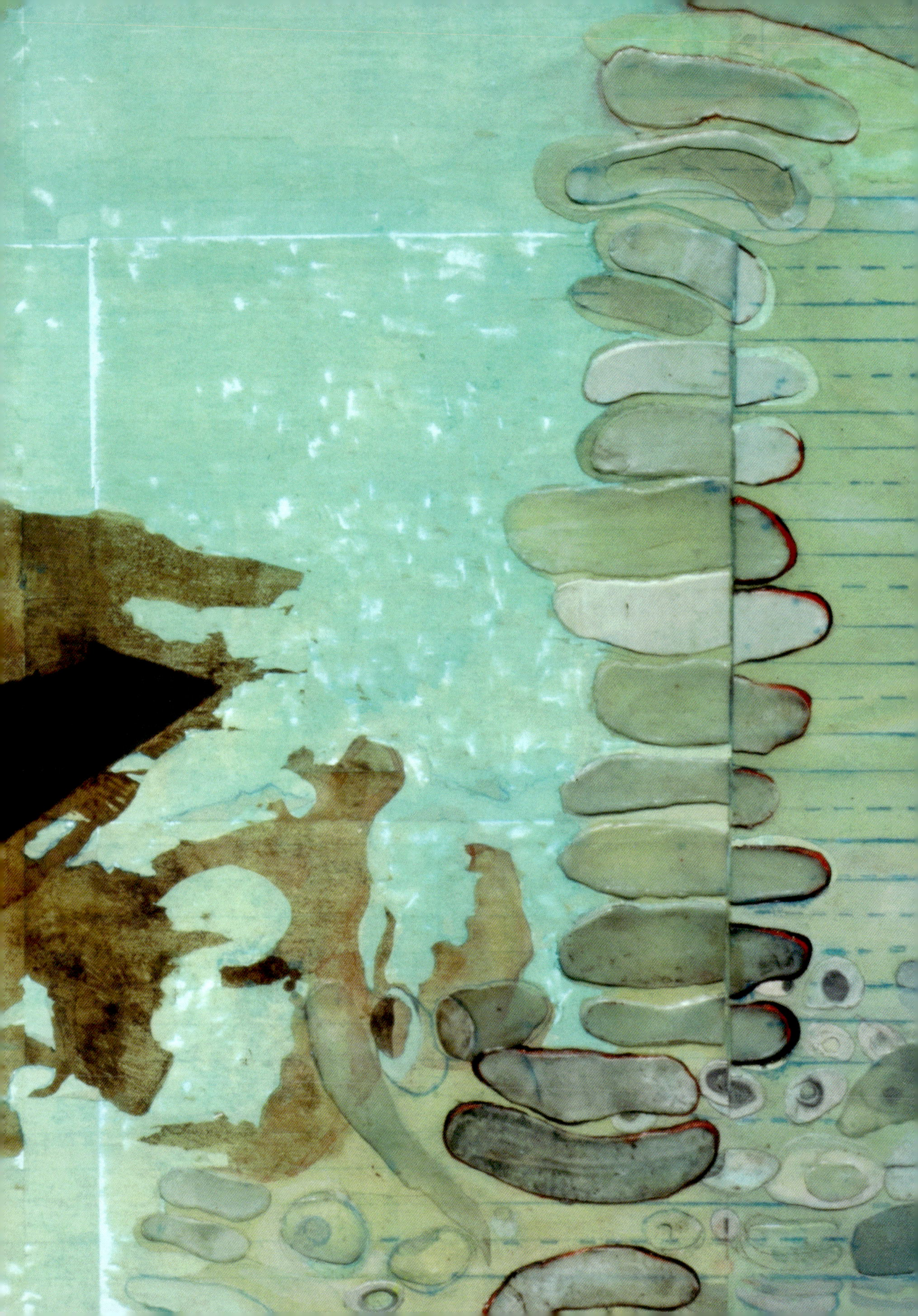

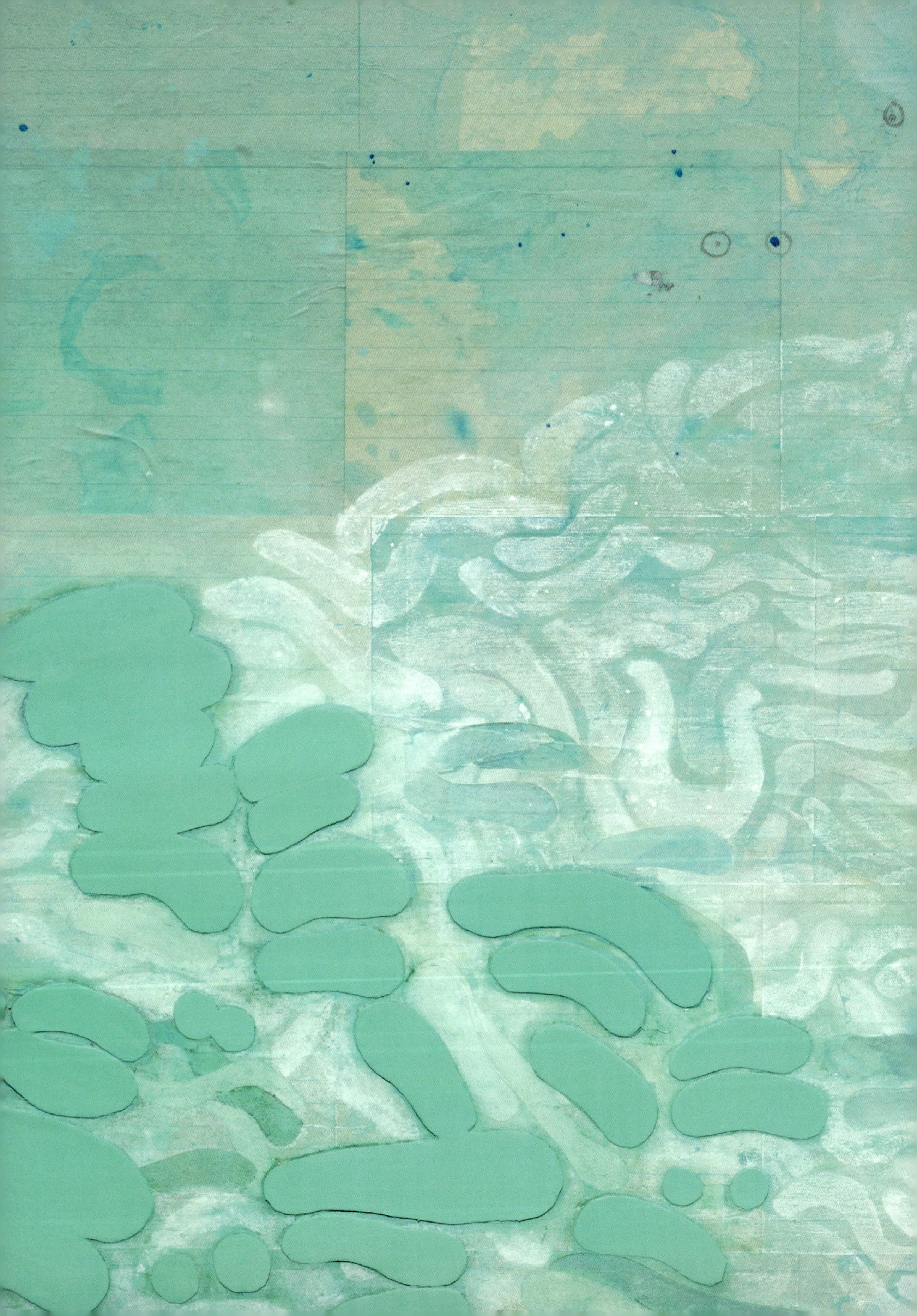

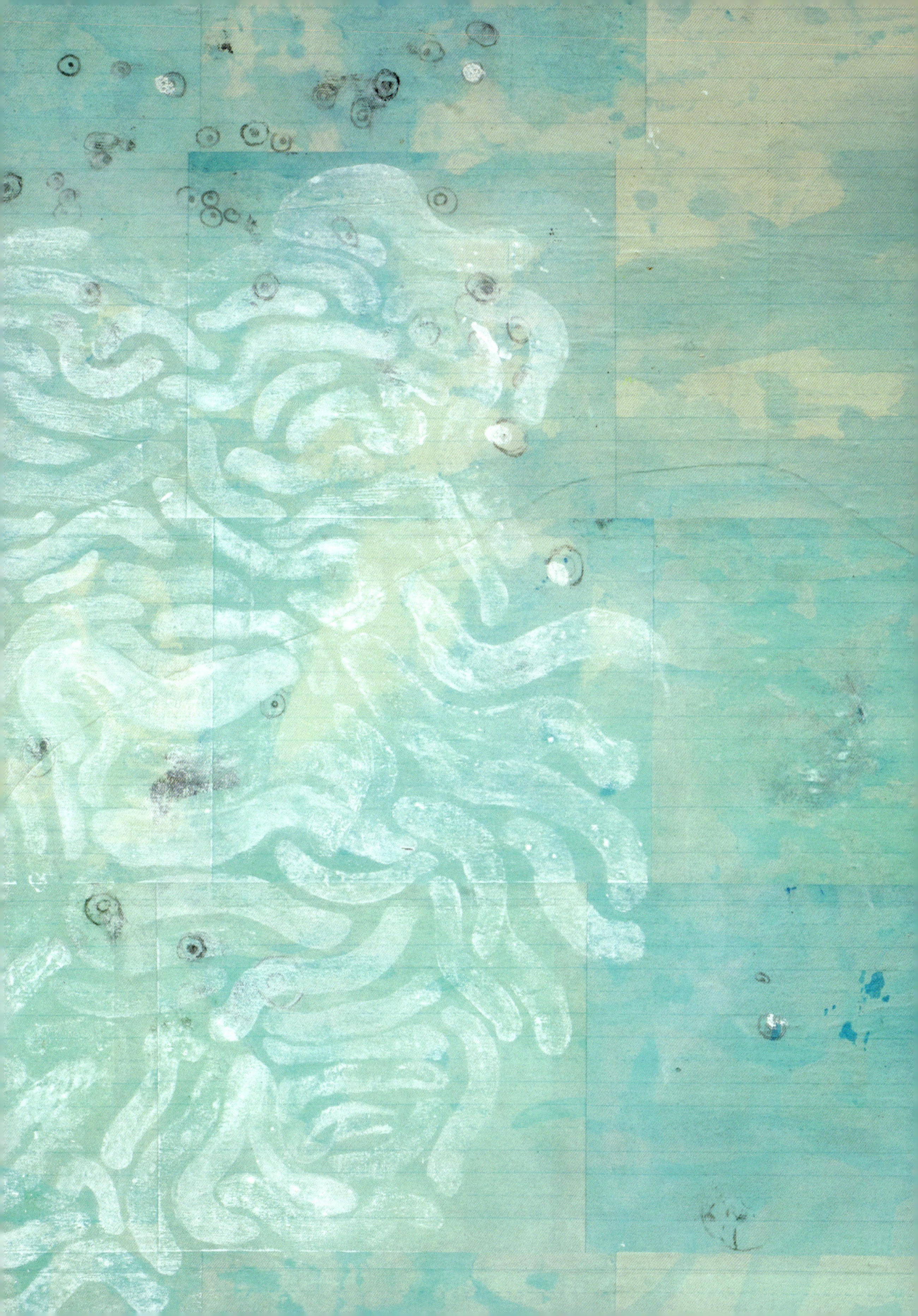

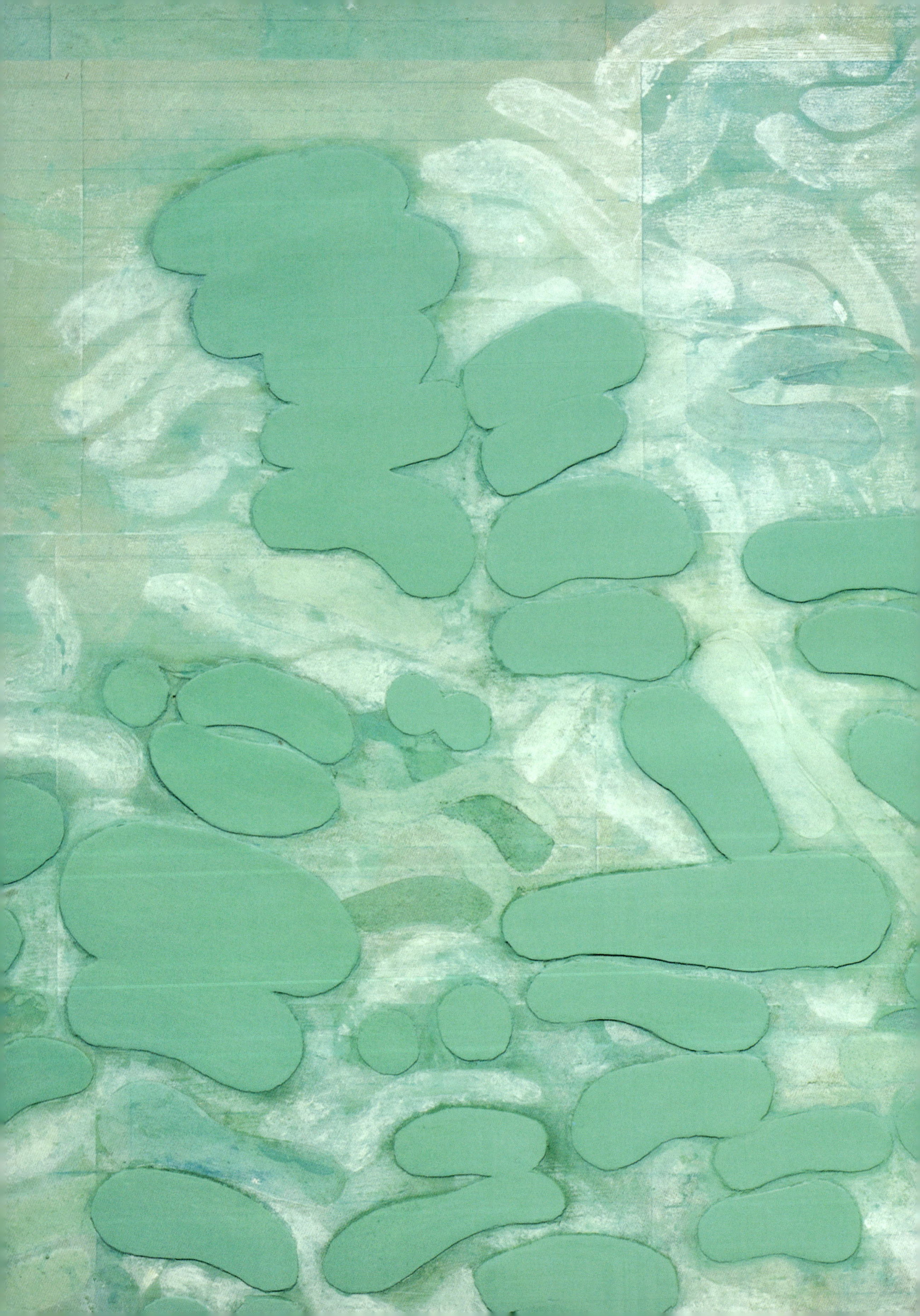

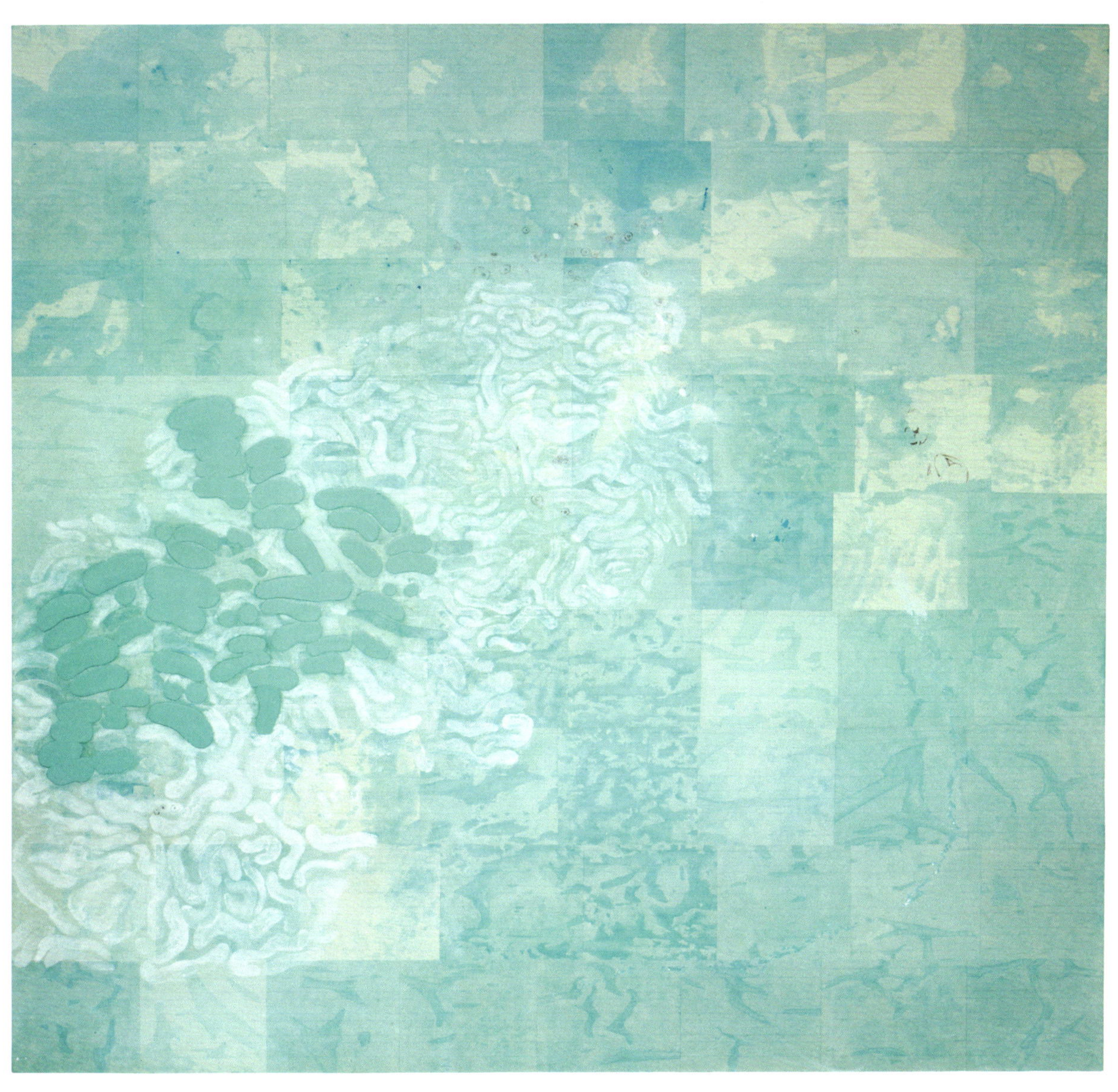

Hydropoly Spores　2017
Oil, ink, and paper on canvas
74 × 79 ½ in　188 × 202 cm

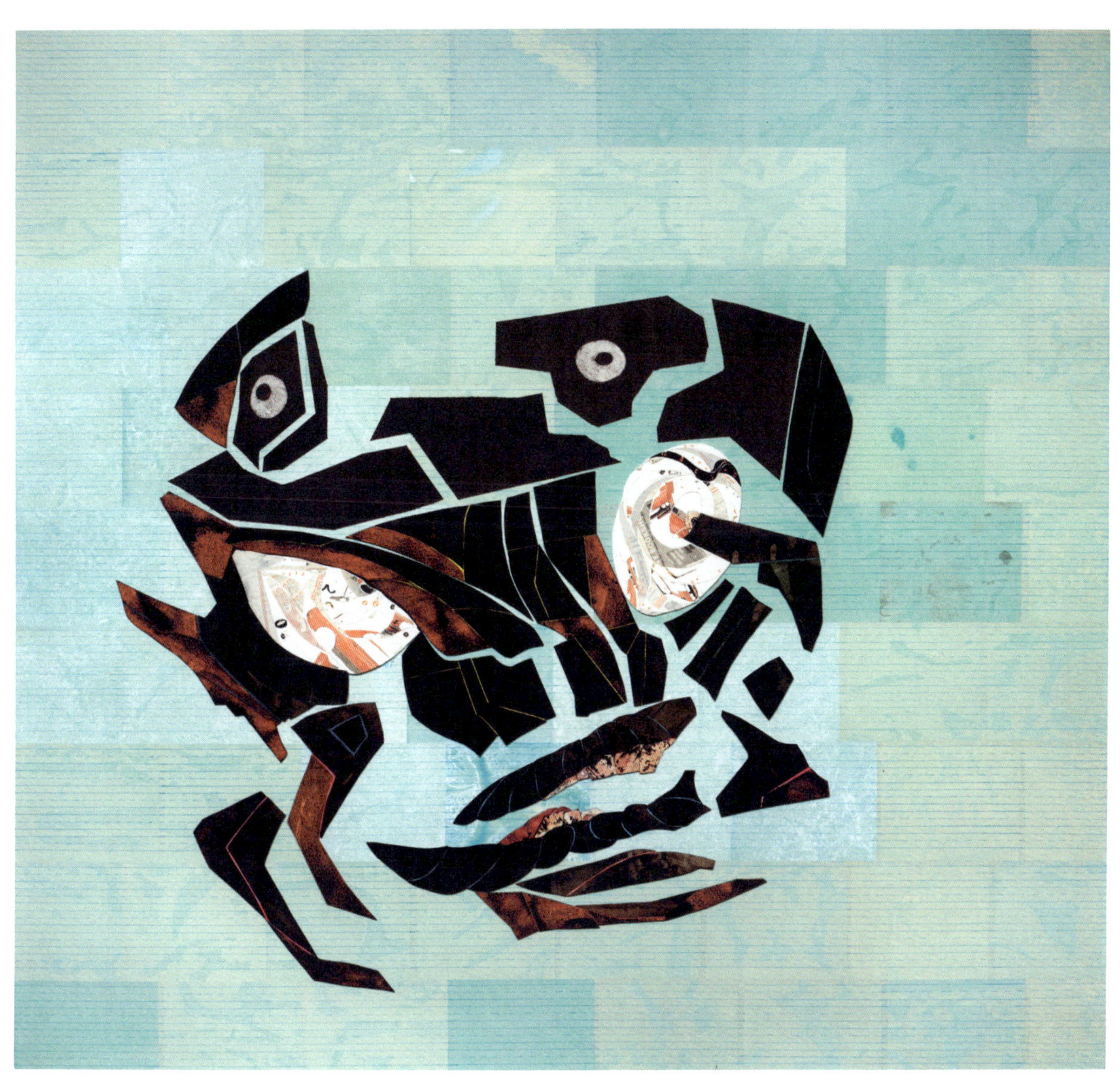

Aquajujidsu   2017
Oil, ink, and paper on canvas
74 × 79 ½ in   188 × 202 cm

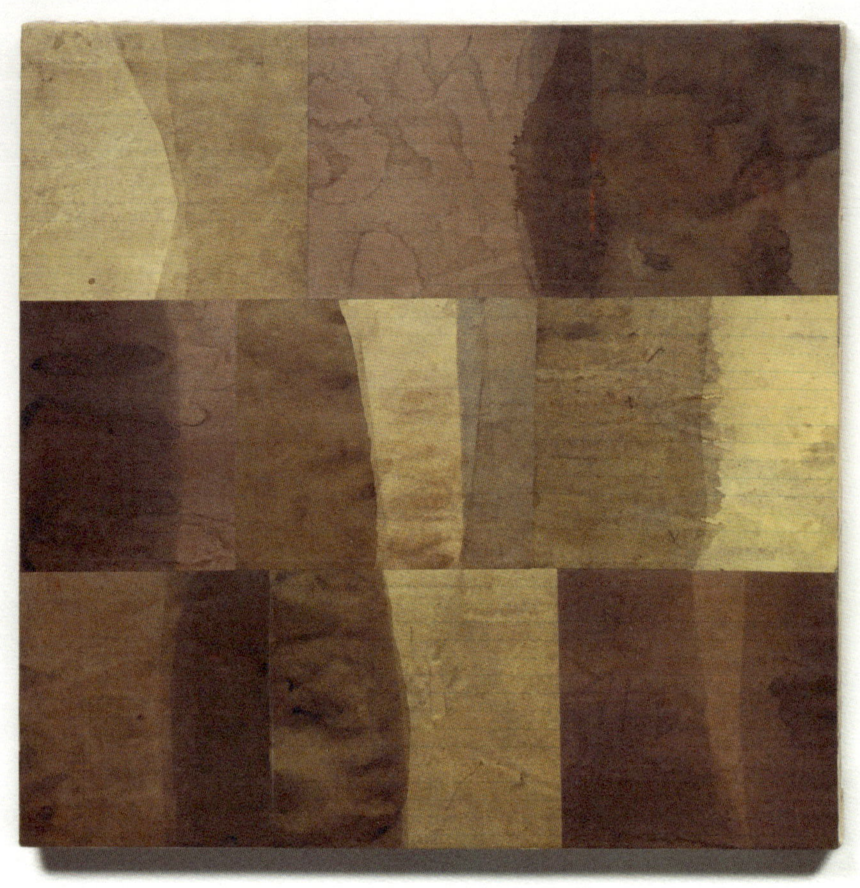

62

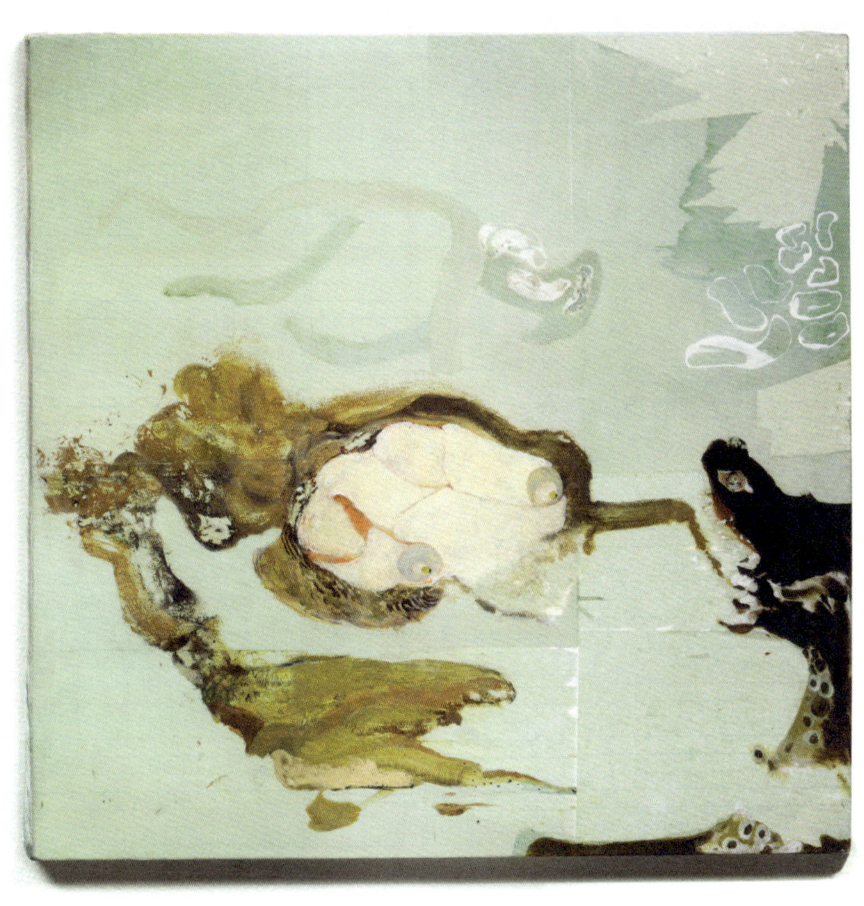

Sea Bed (Sediment)   2017
Oil, ink, and paper on canvas
Each: 24 ⅛ × 24 ¼ × 1 ¾ in   61.2 × 61.5 × 4.5 cm

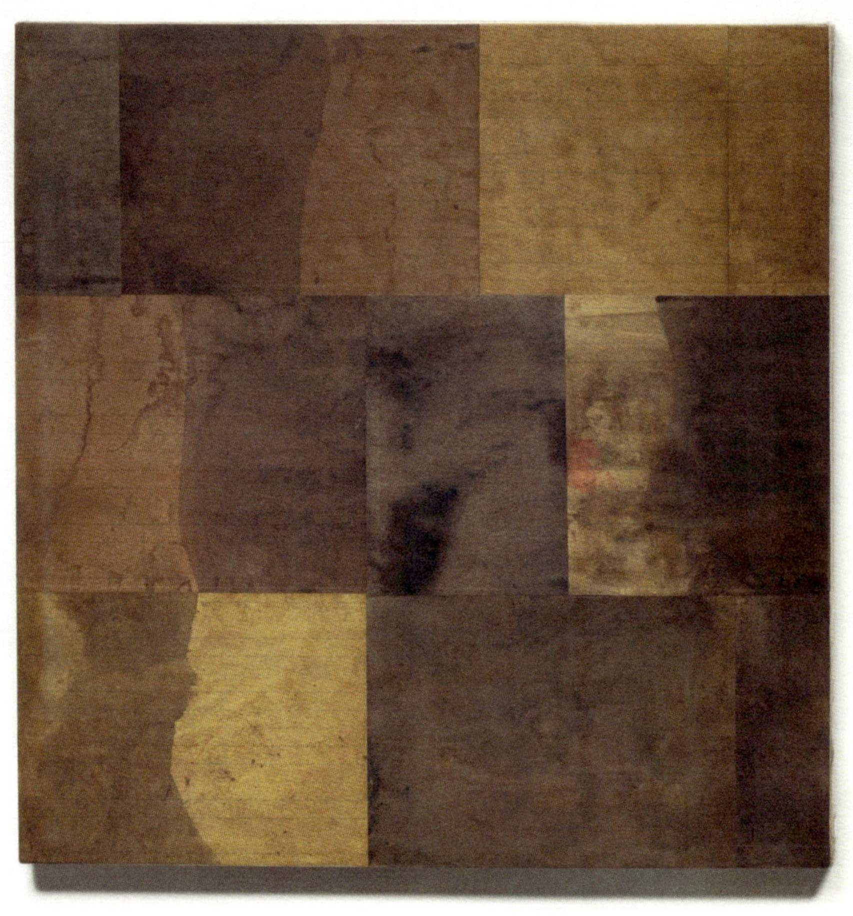

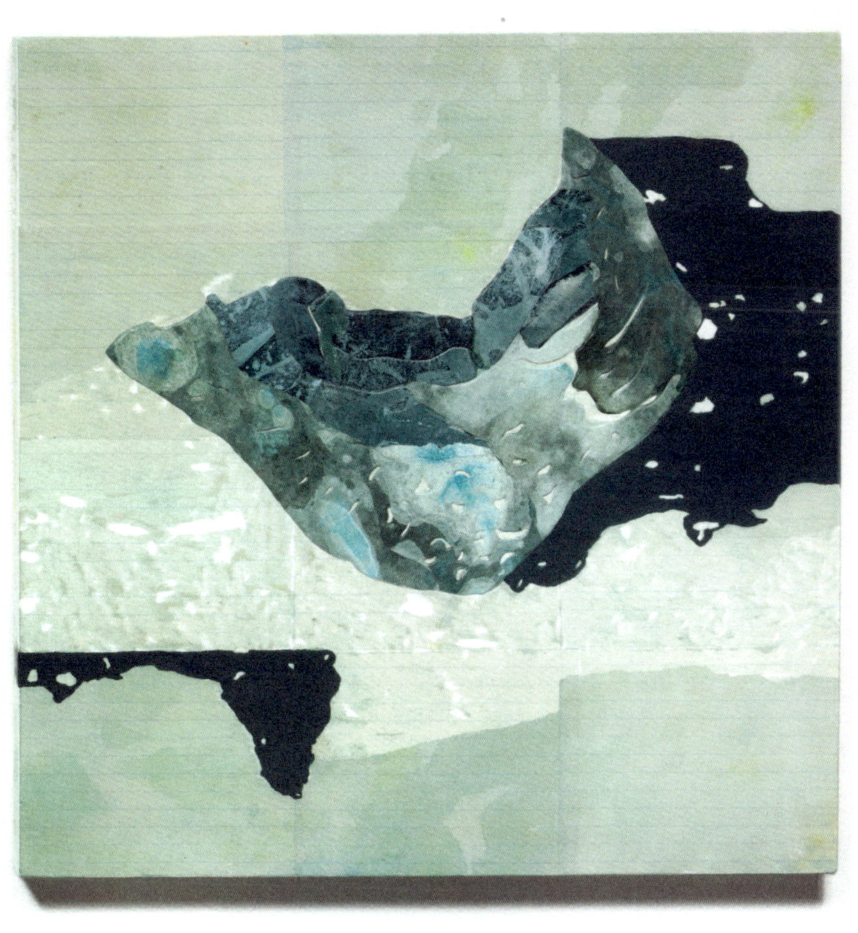

Sea Bed (Grind)   2017
Oil, ink, and paper on canvas
Each: 24 ⅛ × 24 ¼ × 1 ¾ in   61.2 × 61.5 × 4.5 cm

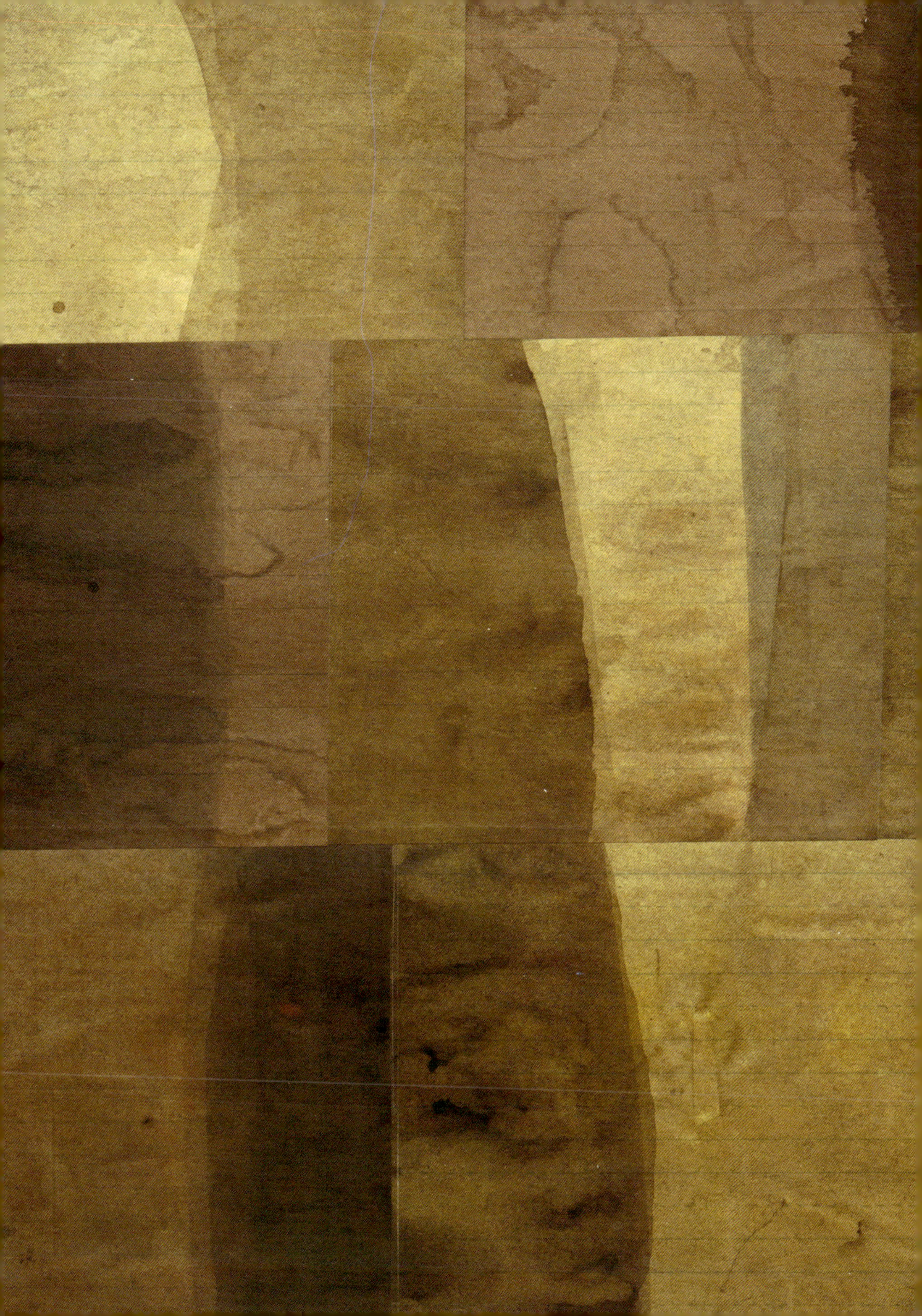

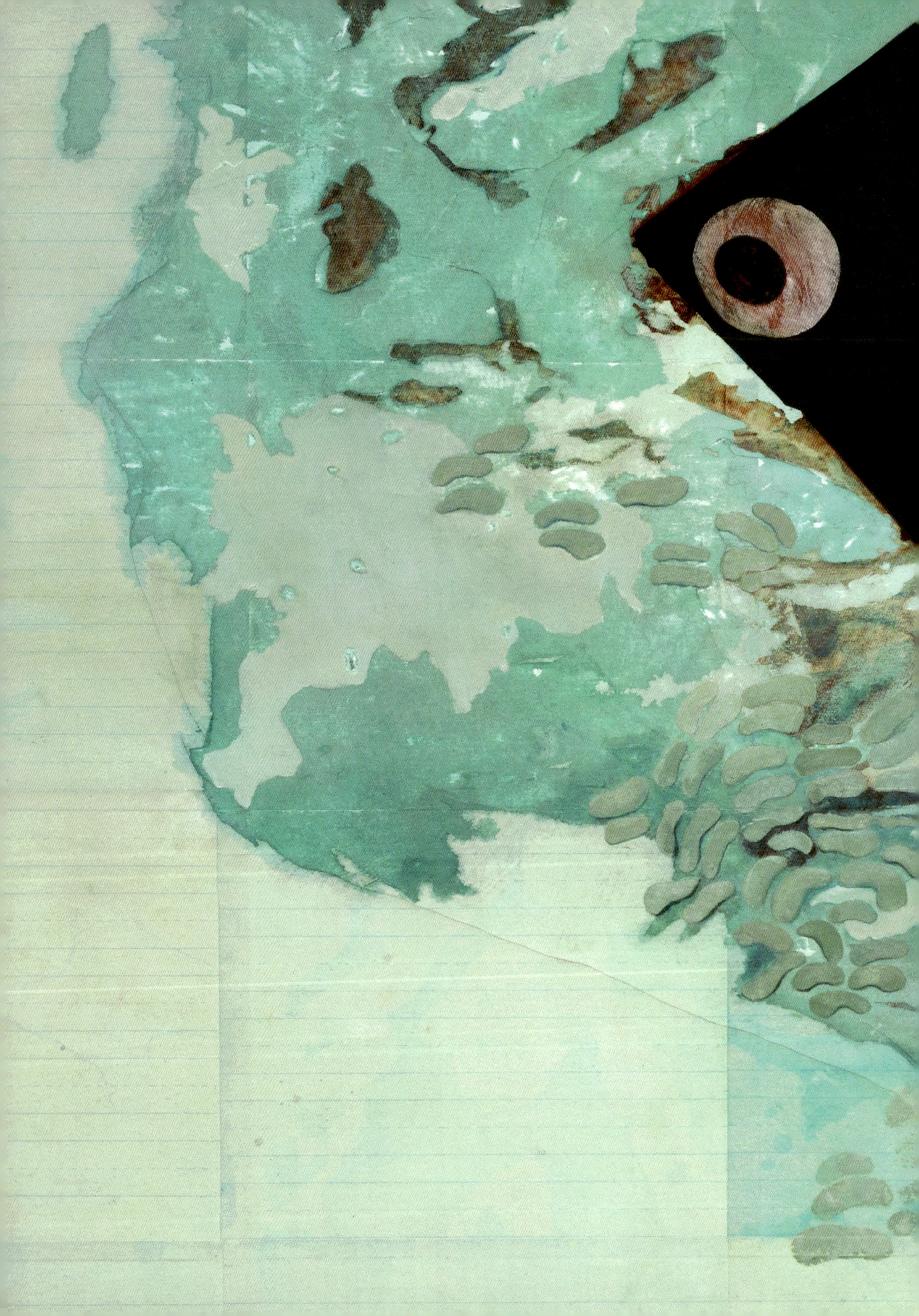

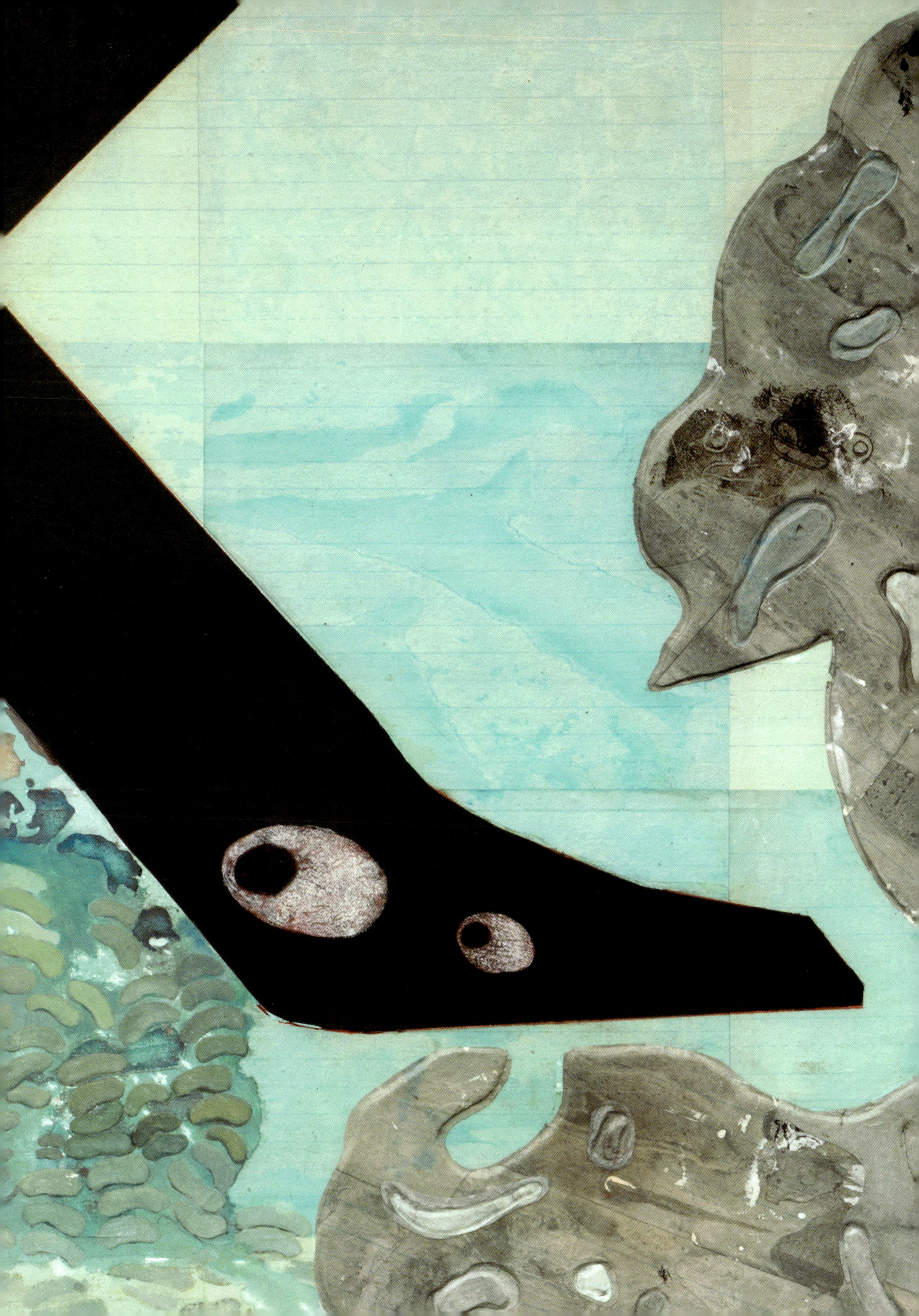

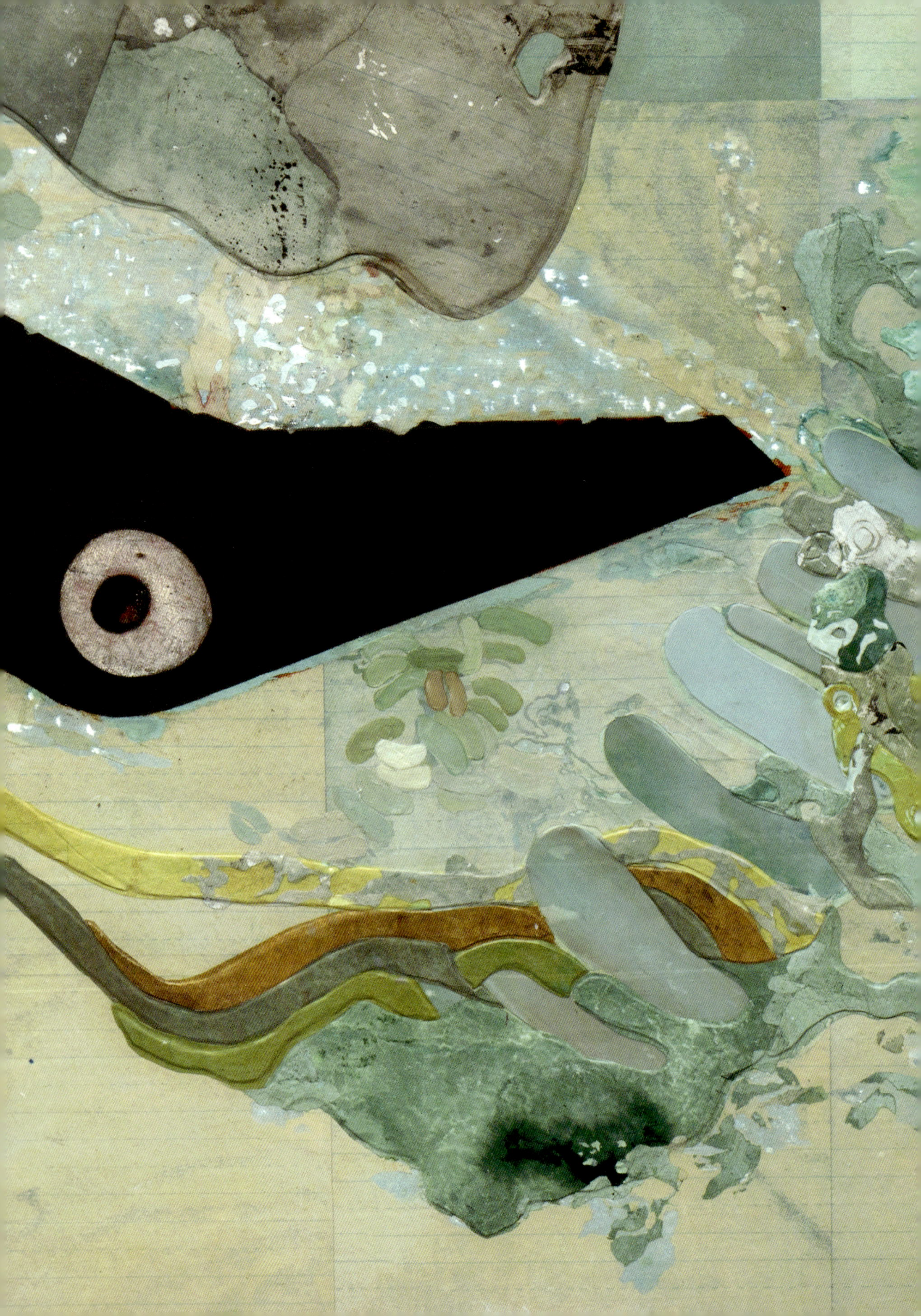

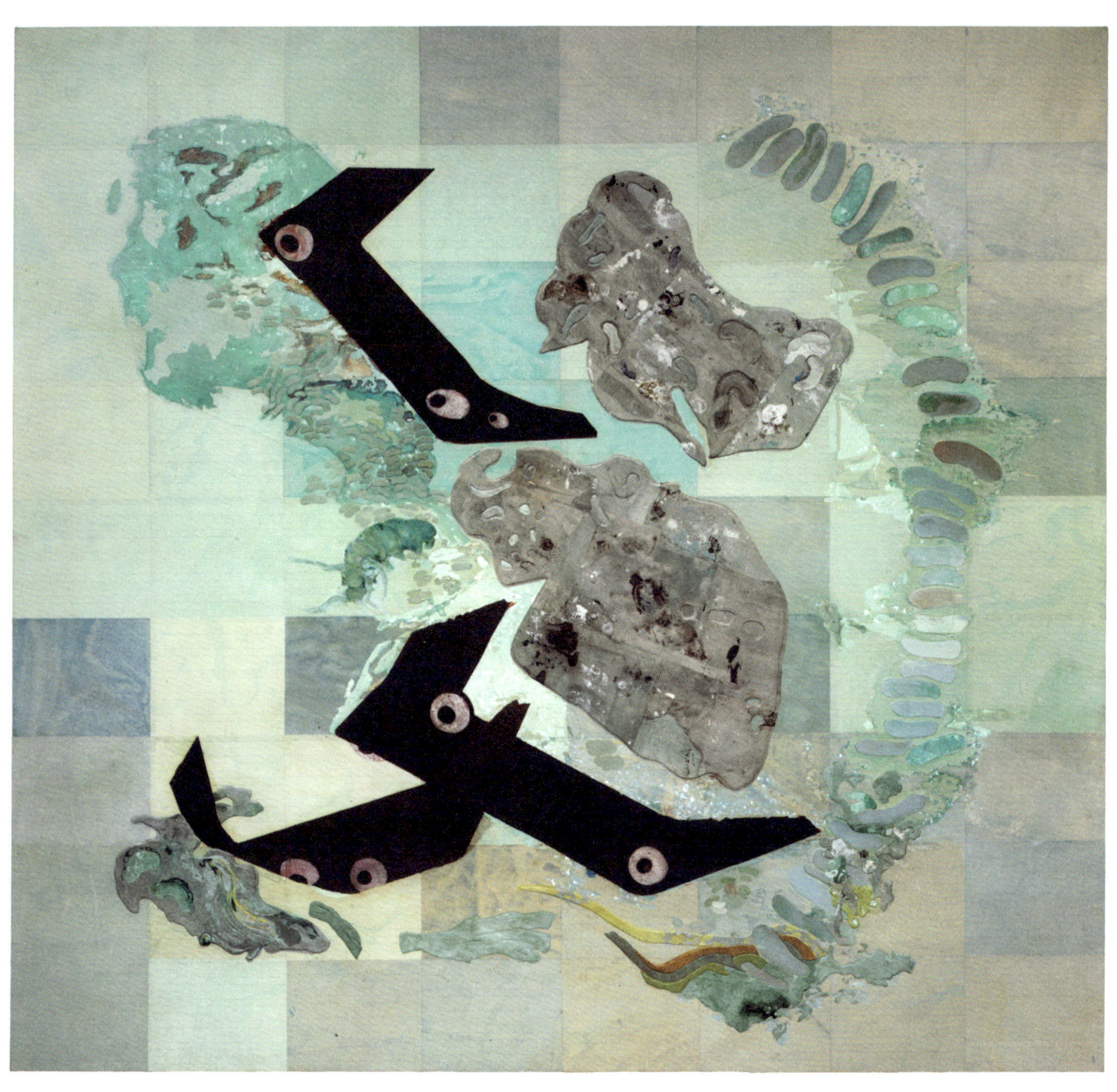

Whale Falls   2017
Oil, acrylic, ink, and paper on canvas
74 × 79 ½ in   188 × 202 cm

I'll dream fast asleep
Philip Hoare

When I was a boy growing up in suburban Southampton, by a
great seaport, my mother used to tell me about the bath in her childhood
home. It was one of those Victorian roll top tubs, deep and sturdy.
And along the side of it, as if to cheer it up, her father – my grandfather –
had painted a great big spouting whale.
I never knew my grandfather; he died before I was born.
I never visited that house. But that bath lingered long in my imagination.
I connected it to the deep dark sea that lay a mile from where we lived,
from whose shore the sound of foghorns would drift into my bedroom as if
the ships were sheep lost in the night. It was the sound of another world,
far beyond mine. Down in those docks – a no man's land that seemed to
belong to neither earth, nor water – crates of bananas were landed from the
distant West Indies with big hairy spiders accidentally imprisoned inside.
The limpid blue of the Caribbean was an exotic impossibility;
I was frightened enough of the steel-grey, freezing English Channel. But the
thought of what lay beneath made me even more afraid. In my imagination,
that spouting whale swam up Southampton Water – alongside all the
glamorous white liners and the functional container ships – and into my
head. I was so fearful of this persistent childhood dream that I didn't even
like taking a bath. The fantastical depths, as we all know, are so much more
profound than the real ones.

*   *   *

The North Sea surges into Rotterdam's Nieuwe Maas, a well-
named waterway since it seems to gather mass with its own inherent
force; a sheer, unstoppable volume. It's from the Maas that all the waters of
Europe seem to pour out to sea; and through which all the sea pours into
Europe. Like the coast near my childhood home, these shores are familiar,
strange, utilitarian places. Put me down here blindfolded and unveil
the seascape, and I'd say we were in New York or Southampton or any
other populous place connected to the water. Here sail the same vast
liners, globally roaming from port to port as if in search of distraction; their
superstructures looming almost as high as the unrelenting contemporary
tower blocks that occupy the Wilhelminakade, the pier that juts out from
Rotterdam's dockhead.
The water taxis, sleek and stubby and black like little whales,
bounce from one quay to another, connecting the watery city. And behind
us, at the head of the Wilhelminakade, sits the defiant Jugendstil glory
of the Hotel New York, a red brick building topped with verdigris domed
towers, which was once the head office of the Holland-Amerika Lijn. From
1906 onwards, its rooms processed the departures of millions of emigrants
headed for North America, all seeking a better life.
On 14 May 1940, the historic centre of Rotterdam was entirely
destroyed by the Luftwaffe. In one night, in an attack lasting fifteen minutes,
nearly a thousand people were killed and 80,000 were made homeless.

The bombs wiped out 250 hectares and 252 streets. In the years of reconstruction that followed after the war – at a time of great movements of people, power, culture, and ideas – Rotterdam was rebuilt in its own image in the way that Theseus's ship, although its timbers were continually replaced, remained Theseus's ship. Was this still Rotterdam, or a future version of it?

The high tide swells and laps around the port as Ellen Gallagher takes us on a high-speed ferry ride. Moving fast through these surging waters is exhilarating, not just because of the rushing spray and the ever-changing panorama of buildings, but because I see them through Ellen's eyes. Born to an Irish-American mother and a father of Cape Verdean parentage, she is also connected to this sea. The fingers of the Atlantic draw a line from Providence, Rhode Island where Ellen grew up – a place she has described as 'all ocean' – to this part of old Europe, where she now feels at home. 'There's always this sense of rebuilding and making', she says, observing that this working-class port looks just like Queens, New York. The port's constant recreation moves hand-in-hand with its people, its history, and its future.

No port stays still, it isn't in its nature. And each port is more linked to other ports than to its homeland. It was from Rotterdam that the Pilgrims set sail for Southampton, bound for New England in 1620. The first thing they saw when they arrived on the shores of Cape Cod (which would become Provincetown harbour), were whales so numerous that the Pilgrims thought they might walk across the bay on the animals' backs. The land from the Hudson River to Rhode Island was a province of the Dutch republic known as New Netherland. New York was New Amsterdam, and the great whaling fleet of the Netherlands would inspire the whalers of the American Republic. In his introduction to Moby-Dick, Melville asserts that the word 'whale' derives from the Dutch wallen, which means to roll, to wallow, as the waters roll and wallow. Melville's own mother was a Gansevoort, and the writer grew up speaking Dutch. 'They were expecting me', says Ellen, as we climb off the boat.

As a child, Ellen recalls being taken across the post-war highway that divided the Cape Verdean community of Providence from the rest of the city, and from the sea that brought them there. Her father, whose parents came from those Atlantic islands off the coast of Africa, insisted that it was their right to do so; to make that reconnection. She tells me that Cape Verdeans, who had first arrived in New England on whaling ships, are now being dispossessed of their neighbourhoods – of their culture itself – by gentrification and 'progress'.

'This doesn't exist by the time I have memory', Ellen says, as she shows me photographs on her iPad of the islands celebrating their festivals in those streets. She recalls the intimate, transatlantic connection with whaling, one of the industries that connected Africa, Europe, and America. The Ernestina, a former whaling ship, undertook her last voyage in 1965, the year Ellen was born. It carried food and money back to the islands' families, to an archipelago so dry that it seemed, as Ellen says, 'a marine extension of the Sahara'. For most of the 20th century, Cape Verdean-Americans were unable to visit their islands, fearing they would be denied re-entry by the American government which had implemented stringent immigration policies. By the time the restrictions were lifted in the 1960s, the two communities seemed irrevocably divided. Now the American streets where these African islanders settled seemed almost as though they were 'haunted by something', Ellen says.

Men in pale caps still stood outside buildings whose meaning and use had changed. They could not be so easily shifted.

*   *   *

Cycles – historical, personal, emotional, and natural – recur in Ellen Gallagher's work. In a world in which new borders are being erased and redrawn, her art is fluid with stories and allusions. It was in Provincetown – which in the 20th century became another kind of colony, dedicated to art – that Ellen saw her first whale, and where, as she has said, water became a character in her life. Now she divides her time between Rotterdam and Red Hook, Brooklyn, sites connected by this same green-grey water; the storied Atlantic, the abused ocean – a conduit for her forebears, and the provocation for her practice.

The sea has a history. The sea is our history. It lurks there, in the back of our minds, even as we turn our collective backs on it, as if it were too awful and too beautiful to contemplate. 'The sea, everywhere the sea,' wrote the Haitian artist Dany Laferrière, 'and no one looking at it'. Those who do look can barely record what they see. In J.M.W. Turner's whaling paintings of the 1840s, a black shape lurches up from the waves like a blunt missile about to be launched, or some terrible thing being born. The image could be biblical or pagan. The blood spurts from the whale like the spermaceti springs from his head (that for which he was hunted gave him his seminal name). The harpoon's line is an umbilical cord, linking life and death.

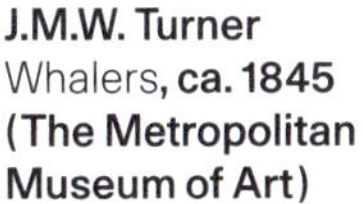

J.M.W. Turner
Whalers, ca. 1845
(The Metropolitan
Museum of Art)

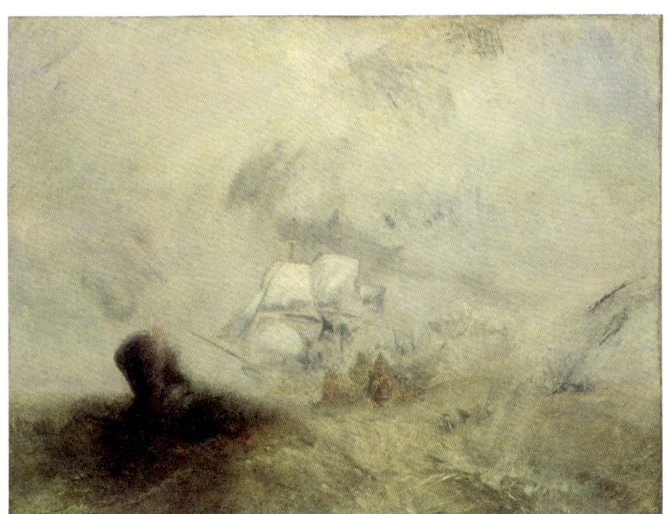

This is the same water in which 133 stolen people bound for Jamaica were drowned in 1781. They had been travelling on the Dutch slave ship Zong (its original name was Zorg, meaning 'care'). On the orders of the British captain, Luke Collingwood, they were chained ankle to ankle and weighed down with iron balls before being thrown through the cabin windows; many were women, some pregnant, others were drowned with their children. Collingwood himself died of fever three days after the Zong reached Jamaica. On arrival, his ship contained only half of the slaves it had collected from Africa. The scene was reimagined in Turner's Slave Ship (1840), in which strange monstrous shapes emerge from the sea as if to claim their prize. As the ship's owners collected their insurance, they left their drowned cargo behind.

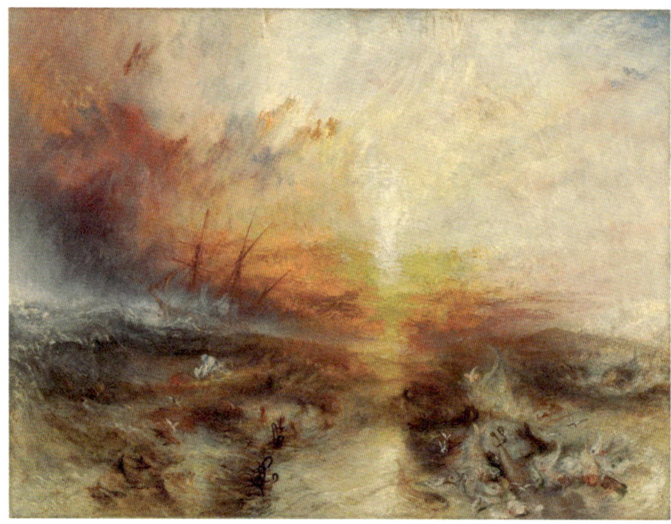

J. M. W. Turner
Slave Ship (Slavers
Throwing Overboard
the Dead and Dying,
Typhoon Coming On),
1840
**(Museum of
Fine Arts, Boston)**

When it was first exhibited in London, Turner's painting became a focal point for the campaign to end slavery. Indeed, the artist was deliberately evoking another extraordinary image, created twenty years earlier. Géricault's giant canvas, The Raft of the Medusa (1818–1819), depicts the terrible aftermath of a ship which was wrecked carrying would-be colonists to Senegal. A lone black figure at the prow of the raft waves a red shirt – seeking rescue, or perhaps signalling revolution. The painting was greeted by public sensation; its true meaning was clear. The historian Julian Michelet declared that 'Our whole society is aboard the raft of the Medusa'. As I write this, I hear news of African migrants being thrown overboard by people smugglers, their hands tied together.

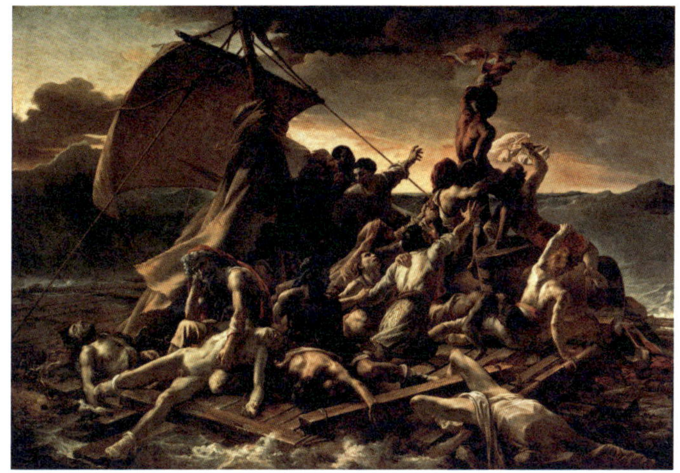

The Atlantic is a freighted sea. It is mapped out by its triangular trade in goods, people, and sugar, a trade in which my own ancestors were involved. The ocean is, in the contemporary critic Kowdo Eshun's phrase, 'a liquid graveyard'. In the 1990s, an electronic duo from Detroit, Drexciya, imagined a watery utopia out of this narrative. They wondered if humans could breathe in water. Could those drowned African slaves have given birth to infants that needed no air? 'Are Drexciyans water breathing, aquatically mutated descendants of those unfortunate victims of human greed?', they wrote. 'Have they been spared by God to teach us or terrorise us? Did they migrate from the Gulf of Mexico to the Mississippi River basin and on to the great lakes of Michigan? Do they walk among us?' This was the future seen in the past. As Eshun says, 'The ships, after all, had landed long ago'.

Logo of Drexciya,
Detroit electronic duo
active from 1992–2002

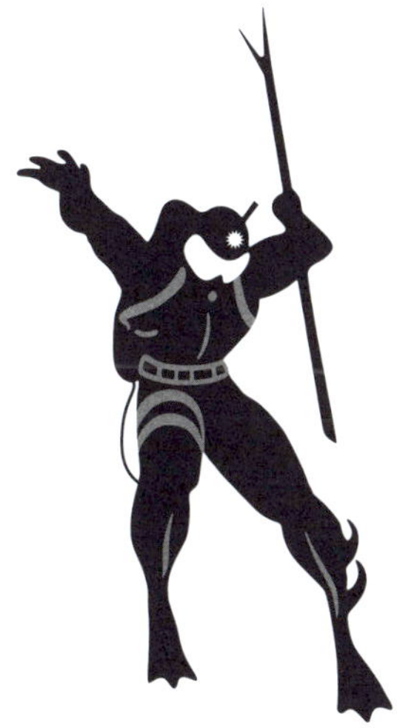

Three years ago in Haiti, I watched as a boat sailed out with a vodou priestess entirely garbed in white, from her turban to her feet. She cast offerings to the lwa – the spirits of the sea – propitiating them, on that Saturday morning, with cigarettes and brandy. A young Haitian told me how, as a boy, he'd been throwing stones into the sea on an apparently deserted beach when an elderly man appeared out of nowhere and asked him to stop what he was doing: he was disturbing the people who lived under the water. The same young man also told me of a remote cave on the north of the island, where vodouisants promised their followers that if they entered, they would emerge on the other side in their ancestral African home.

Ellen Gallagher
Dew Breaker, 2015

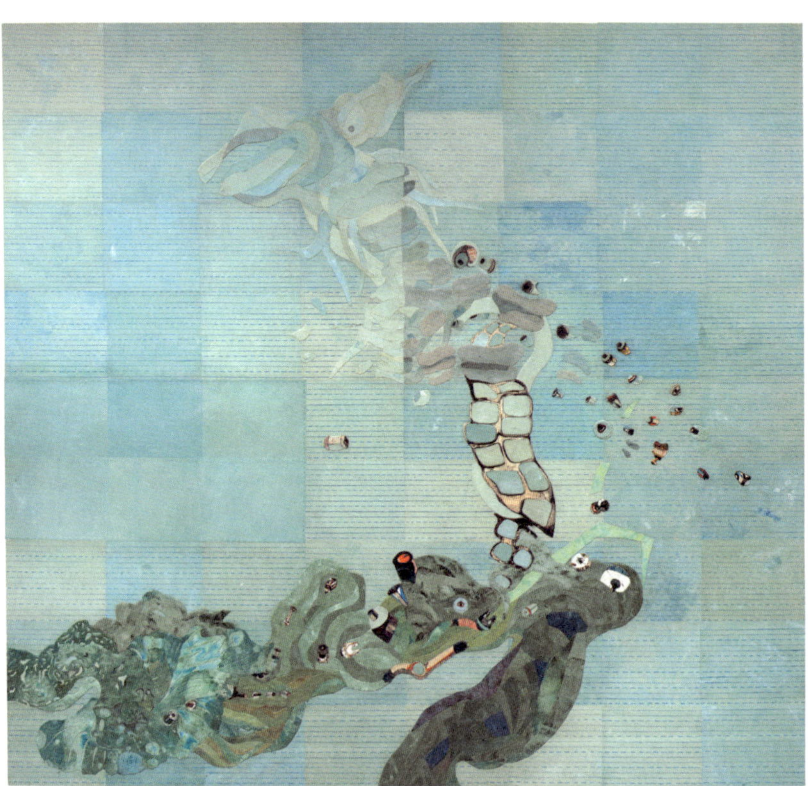

The oceans are stained by what we have done to them. And here in the Netherlands – the never lands – the ocean's porous power is symbolised by the fact that so much of this country lies below sea level; as if its inhabitants were amphibious.

In the evening, Ellen and I drive with the Dutch artist Edgar Cleijne to Zeeland, leaving the estuarine sprawl of Rotterdam – with its vast petrol refinery towers burning off their excess gas – and heading out towards the sea. This is a fractured land, fragmented into flat islands. It was from Middelburg, Zeeland's capital, that the Zorg sailed in search of slaves in the late 18th century. But two centuries earlier, in December 1520, Albrecht Dürer came here, hoping to see a whale.

It was an extraordinary expedition. Dürer, celebrated for his studies of animals, probably wanted to draw the unfortunate creature, or he may have had visions of collecting its ivory teeth for his cabinet of curiosities back in Nüremberg. 'At Zierikzee in Zeeland, a whale has been stranded by a high tide and a gale of wind', he wrote in his journal. 'It is much more than 100 fathoms long and no man living in Zeeland has seen one even a third as long as this is. The fish cannot get off the land; the people would gladly see it gone, as they fear the great stink, for it is so large that they say it could not be cut in pieces and the blubber boiled down in half a year'.

100 fathoms – 600 feet – would certainly be the measure of a prodigious beast, and not that of any living animal. But this monster (however huge) eluded the artist's pursuit: 'Early on Monday we started again by ship, and went by Veere and Zierikzee and tried to get sight of the great fish, but the tide had carried him off again'. Dürer was, however, shown another fearsomely-toothed creature, a walrus, occasionally seen on the more northerly coasts of the North Sea. This rare specimen, far from its icy home (where it was believed to climb icebergs using its tusks and fall asleep whilst hanging in that precarious position) was, as Dürer wrote, 'taken in the Netherlandish sea ... and was 12 Brabant ells long and had four feet'. (Another artist's exaggeration: a Brabant ell was the distance from the armpit to the finger tips – about 70 centimetres or 27 inches, and male walruses reach 3.6 metres, or 11 feet in length.) Dürer would later reimagine this whiskery creature as a fabulous dragon.

Albrecht Dürer
Walrus, **1521**
(British Museum, London)

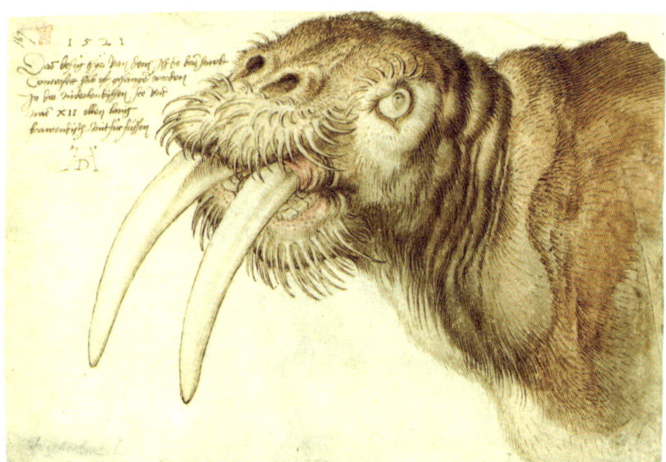

These flat shores, stretching back from the sea – weighed down and almost sinking with history – witnessed a strange deputation of such behemoths, as if summoned by some obscure signal. In 1577, a veritable fleet of sperm whales stranded on the southern Netherlands, spilling out of the foamy waves. And in 1598, further up the coast, beyond The Hague, another whale appeared (to be depicted in etchings and even on Delftware), its deflated body outlined in the characteristic deep blue Dutch glaze. Another sperm whale which appeared in 1601 was drawn in extraordinary detail by Jan Saenredam – in a style somewhat reminiscent of Dürer's Melencolia I – alongside a series of images showing, amongst other omens, a comet bearing the plague striking Amsterdam.

In *Moby-Dick*, Melville, the erstwhile Dutchman, claims no one produced accurate images of whales until the early 19th century. The artistic responses to the many strandings on this coast – a country with such a fine art tradition – disprove this. The suicidal whales could have made no better choice for the site of their self-sacrifice, knowing their final act would be so well represented.

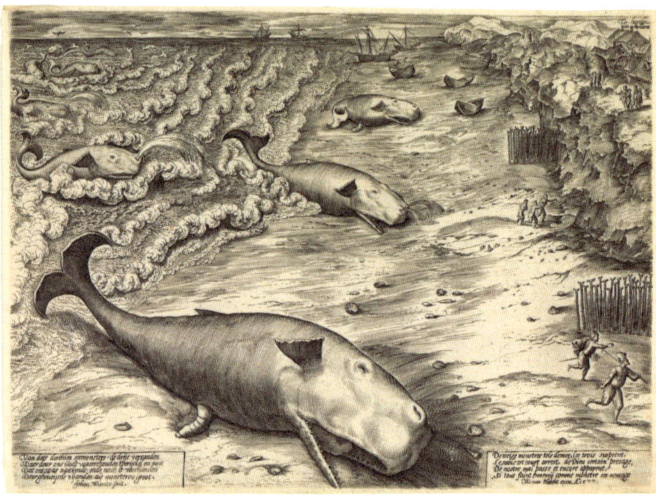

Jan Wierix
Three Beached Whales,
1577

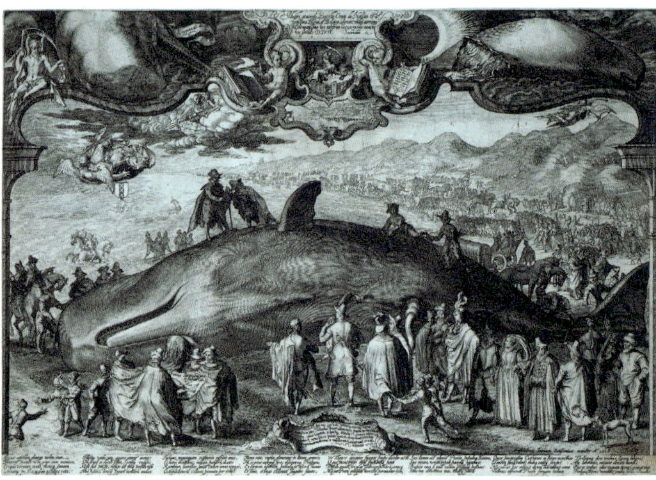

Jan Saenredam
Whale beached at
Beverwijk, 1602

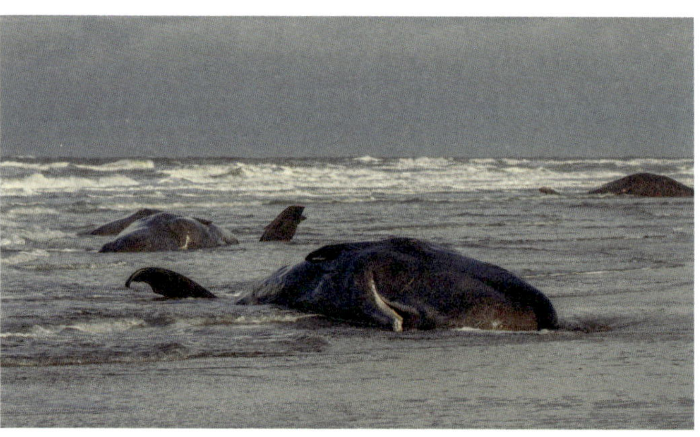

Five sperm whales
beached at Texel,
north of Amsterdam, 2016.
Photo: Jeroen Hoekendijk

Such exquisitely rendered scenes of animals that were taken as signs – as much as were plague-bearing comets trailing in the sky – are poignantly counterpointed by a remarkable modern stranding of 29 sperm whales around the shores of the North Sea in January 2016, possibly the result, as new research indicates, of solar storms that disrupted their geomagnetic navigation. The Dutch researcher and photographer Jeroen Hoekendijk made the journey to see five of these animals lying in the surf on the beach at Texel, north of Amsterdam. They were still alive. Hoekendijk's image of the whales is freighted with a terrible power when one reads his account of the cetaceans still trying to draw breath as they suffocate under their own enormous weight, having forsaken the element which had supported their wondrous bulk. At least four of these whales, once dissected, were found to have large pieces of plastic in their bellies.

The media attention greeting this deputation from the deep took it as a new omen of our spoiled oceans. Since the 1960s, we have accepted the whale as an emblem of a threatened nature, and its omnipresence in our culture speaks, perhaps, to our sense of guilt. In a remarkable echo of this presence and absence, an unassuming beach scene by the 17th-century artist Hendrick van Anthonissen was recently discovered to be concealing, under an overpainted portion, the shape of a stranded sperm whale. Thus revealed by artistic forensics, it was as if Dürer's intended subject had suddenly reappeared, out of history.

Hendrick van
Anthonissen
View of Scheveningen
Sands, 1641
(The Fitzwilliam Museum)
[before and after
conservation]

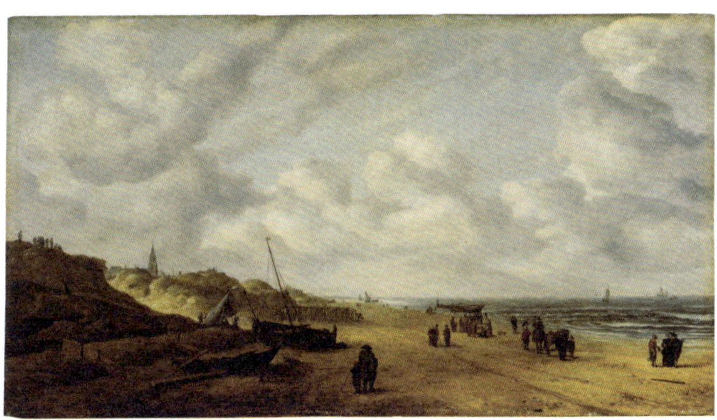

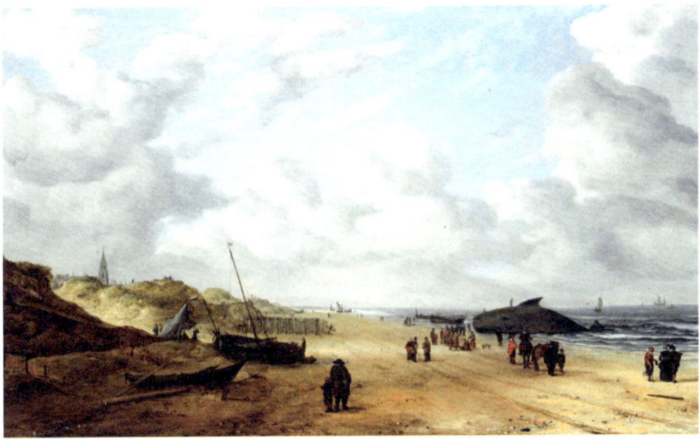

Yet we only have Dürer's word that the 1520 whale ever existed at all. Guido Keijl, a modern historian of Dutch whales and whale strandings, has been unable to find any other contemporary account (and as Hoekendijk notes, everything else about the story is just 'assumption and interpretation'). Dürer only ever drew a whale in his head. It was as if the animal were paradoxically too big, too mythic, and too elusive be recorded. It reminded me of the French name for the sperm whale, a more elegant nomenclature, cachalot, which to me reads as a play on words: cache à l'eau – to hide in the water.

Zeeland, too, is both here and not here. It expresses its own state of paradox in its name – Sea Land – a place of water and islands, and Holland's least populated area. The sea which makes this land so fertile also makes it deadly. In 1953, in an apocalyptic event that rivalled the airborne disaster of thirteen years before, spring tides and storms conspired to overwhelm the dykes, inundating the fragile, tentative land. Nearly two thousand died in the Netherlands, most of them in Zeeland. On the way here, Edgar, who has inherited his parents' memories of that time, tells us of the many people lost that night, people who were taken away by the waves and never came back, and of the domesticated animals that drowned or floated off, without an ark to save them.

On the other side of the island that was almost entirely flooded that night – the same island where Dürer had sought his whale, and which is shaped a little like a whale itself – we drive past the houses of Bruinisse. Where other houses might have tall hedges, these have protective dykes, green walls against the water. Their windows are bare of conventional lace curtains, in the Calvinist tradition of having nothing to hide. But perhaps the inhabitants seek to let the light into places that are sunk below sea level. Or maybe they need to keep an eye open for the water.

We follow one of the bulwarks that holds the sea at bay. Climbing up and over the grassy dyke, where brown hares run, we find a perfect shallow expanse of water laid before us, part salt, part sweet. It is deserted and private, curtained by green and blue. A little wooden jetty leads out into the stillness. I launch off into it, submerging my body in the summer-warm sea. There is nothing else in this brief moment. Ellen stands on the shore, looking out to sea; Edgar climbs over the rocks, foraging for seaweed; I swim. We are caught in and out of time.

Inland sea view at
Bruinisse
Photo: Ellen Gallagher

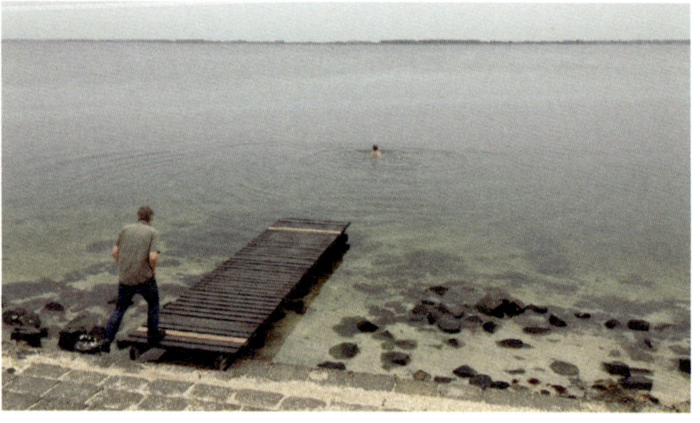

Suddenly, out of nowhere, three teenagers arrive. They stand there, staring and wide-eyed, transfixed like Melville's 'water-gazers'. The boy tells Ellen they sometimes see 'sea dogs' here – not walruses, but seals – looking back at them with their big Labrador eyes. 'It makes you want to cry', he says.

The water makes children of us all. Ellen tells me that in a nearby waterway she and Edgar once saw bruinvissen – porpoises – swimming. A group of teenage girls cycling past abandoned their bikes and their 21st-century sophistication and ran over to coo at the sight of the sportive cetaceans.

Later, in a nearby restaurant, the waiter brings a plate to our table. Laid on it is a fresh schol, or plaice. Like the whale and the walrus, it is a specimen Dürer would have admired. The flat fish glistens with the sea, the orange spots on its mottled brown body like the fingerprints of a saint. The waiter holds it before us, offering it up for the delectation of his customers. When Dürer painted his famous hare, he recorded the square panes of a window reflected in its eyes. But this creature's mouth dribbles snot-like spit, and the light in its eyes has long since been extinguished.

*　*　*

The sea inundates our imaginations, time- and shape-shifting, challenging what is there and what is not. It is a protean, transmutative, queer place. Jellyfish, one of the oldest organisms in the sea, change sex during their life spans, drifting as they do through the world's oceans, as they have done for four hundred million years. Some species are colonies within colonies: the Portuguese man o' war, for instance, with its vivid purple frill and varicose-vein tentacles, is in fact a community of zooids or polyps that function as one, as they are blown about the ocean under a gas-filled bladder. Phantasmagorical, neither plant or animal, composed mostly of water – and therefore nothing and everything – jellyfish are the great survivors. These antediluvian colonists have outlived five extinctions and may well outlive the sixth, through which we are living and in which we are complicit.

Our age of the Anthropocene has achieved its own transformations. By the middle of this century there will be more plastic than fish in the sea. We will be eating plastic, just as ninety per cent of seabirds now consume the same stuff. Meanwhile, our contraceptive drugs – which might save the world from too many more of us – turn male fish female. We are imposing our model on the world's oceans. Turn, then, to the womb in which you and I began, the little sea in which we swam, listening to the world through the salty amniotic fluid in our mother's belly, as we developed residual gills and fins. We might unfurl as other beings entirely, fish or whales or humans, depending on an arbitrary slip of genes or genders; a liminal whim.

That is the first barrier we break through: those safe, warm waters. Everything else is crisis. For centuries it was believed that a child born with the amniotic membrane over its face would be protected by this 'caul' from drowning since it had already survived a sort of suffocation.

Preserved cauls became talismans, conferring that protection on anyone who owned them. In Charles Dickens' watery and autobiographical book, David Copperfield is born 'veiled', only to discover that his caul is later auctioned for ten pounds, leaving him strangely bereft, as if a part of himself had been sold off.

One of Ellen's images stays with me (the heir, in my head, to that whale on my grandfather's bath). It is of a decaying baleen whale, slowly swaying and swinging upside-down through the depths till it comes to rest on the sea bed (a phrase which itself suggests a sort of dark comfort). There it will become a new eco-system in its own right. This is birth in reverse, death in life, the beginning of the end of a beginning.

Whale falls occur when dead whales drop into the bathyal or abyssal zone, deeper than one thousand metres, down to the ocean floor. Up to 200 species feed on the remains – an eclectic gathering of eerie, otherly creatures: giant isopods, squat lobsters, bristleworms, hagfish and sleeper sharks. 'The very deep did rot: O Christ!' as Samuel Taylor Coleridge wrote in The Rime of the Ancient Mariner, as if he'd personally descended in an 18th-century diving bell, or in an opiated nightmare. ' ... Yea, slimy things did crawl with legs / Upon the slimy sea'.

Ellen's work was created for her Osedax series, named after the worms which exist on rotting whales (osedax being the Latin for 'bone-eating'). For other species too, a dead whale is the exclusive centre of their life cycle, the decaying blubber and bones all they will ever know (if they can be said to know at all). Far from the sun, they might as well be on another planet; yet the release of energy from that carcase, that what-was-a-whale, is part of the same process from which the whale gathered its energy while it was still living. The sun that raised the phytoplankton fed the zooplankton that fed the sand eels that fed the whale. The same cycle sequesters large amounts of carbon from the atmosphere, storing it for thousands of years. Men deconstructed whales for their own purposes: to yield oil, heat, and light from animals that lived in the cold dark depths. The human thirst for energy has resulted in a changed climate; the dead whale seems to repair it. There is something angelic in this fall into the darkness. In the leviathan's death, there is a ritual renewal, an assertion of the natural world from which we have done our best to absent ourselves, even as we adversely affect it. Our ignorance of the sea is historic and monumental: when the Irish saint Brendan the Navigator was sailing across the Atlantic, he and his fellow monks landed on an island; it was only when they lit a fire that the great whale on which they were perched began to sink beneath them. If living whales resemble archipelagoes, encrusted with barnacles and all but growing trees on their backs, a single dead whale is a sunken island, a world in micro-macrocosm, in the way that Ellen's art is micro- and macrocosmic, her curlicue reefs as atolls within atolls, colonies inside colonies, carved and etched and mapped as much as drawn and collaged and painted.

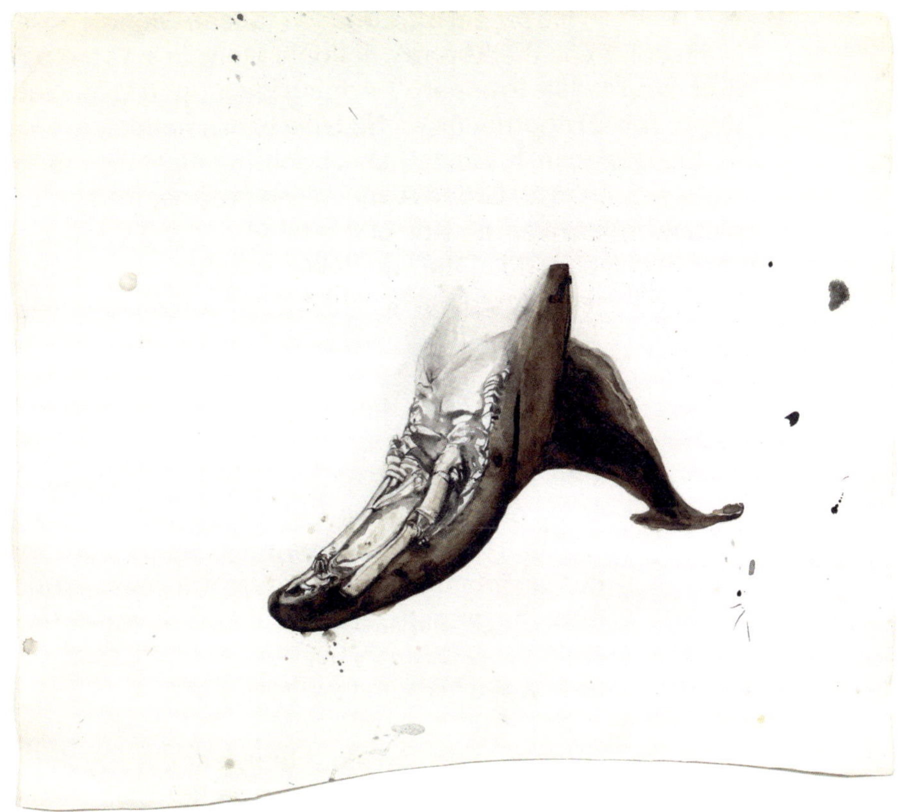

It is 'my version of scrimshaw', says Gallagher. She draws with her scalpel like an anatomist on living skin. Her work might be the product of an 18th-century naturalist as much as it is a future vision – geographical, emblematical, contoured, excavated. The artist's eye zooms in and out synoptically, from her hand to infinity. Dark masks leer out at you from the yeasty sea. Like Turner, whose paintings fed voraciously on the energy created by art and science – disciplines as yet undivided by our disastrous schisms – so Ellen circles the world outside her watery window, drawing it in.

In The Tempest, Shakespeare's last, enigmatic play, the shape-shifting spirit Ariel reports that the opening storm – conjured up by Prospero on his island of strange noises and strange beings – has taken the life of a prince. His royal body has sunk, acquiring immortality in the process.

Those are pearls that were his eyes;
Nothing of him that doth fade,
But doth suffer a sea-change
Into something rich and strange.

In this Renaissance science fiction – which, deriving as it does from England's colonial ventures, has been seen as the dramatist's 'American play' – humans are transformed by the sea, like the Drexciyans; mutating from stolen people into something rich and strange.[1]

In his recent introduction to Jean Giono's novel Melville, Edmund White observes that Giono's fictional Melville 'has the power to summon all of nature – like Prospero'.[2] Adding layer upon layer, delving down deeper only to reveal another layer, Melville was a magician-prophet who saw the future-past in his leviathanic book. In one of the most dreamy episodes in Moby-Dick, 'The Grand Armada', he proposes a sort of aquatopia. Ishmael looks over the side of a whale-boat and sees, in a stilled sea water 'lake', into the world of the whale. He watches as mother gives birth to her calf, the newborn still attached by its umbilical cord as she brings it to the surface to breathe:

> But far beneath this wondrous world upon the surface, another and still stranger world met our eyes as we gazed over the side. For, suspended in those watery vaults, floated the forms of the nursing mothers of the whales ... The lake, as I have hinted, was to a considerable depth exceedingly transparent; and as human infants while suckling will calmly and fixedly gaze away from the breast ... even so did the young of these whales seem looking up towards us, but not at us, as if we were but a bit of Gulf-weed in their new-born sight.

Ishmael feels unaccountably affected by this sight. It is a transcendental scene, perhaps the first description in literature of whales being watched for their own sake. It sends him into metaphysical transports:

> Some of the subtlest secrets of the seas seemed divulged to us in this enchanted pond. We saw young Leviathan amours in the deep. And thus, though surrounded by circle upon circle of consternation and affrights, did these inscrutable creatures at the centre freely and fearlessly indulge in all the peaceful concernments; yea, serenely reveled in dalliance and delight. But even so, amid the tornadoes Atlantic of my being, do I myself still for ever centrally disport in mute calm; and while ponderous planets of unwaning woe revolve round me, deep down and deep inland there I still bathe me in eternal mildness of joy.

Meanwhile, Ishmael's partner, the tattooed Queequeg – the first fully formed person of colour in Western fiction – has equally transcendent origins. He is also a royal prince, 'a native of Kokovoko, an island far away to the West and South. It is not down in any map; true places never are'. Like the island whale, this 'noble savage' embodies a tropical Arcadia, his handsome flesh tattooed by a whale tooth, having undergone his own sea change.[3]

In 'The Castaway' chapter in Moby-Dick, we follow another transformation: that of Ahab's cabin boy Pip, an African American from Connecticut who has the misfortune to fall not once but twice into the water. The first time, Pip is caught in the line which has to be cut to save him, but in the process, the whale is lost. 'A whale will sell for thirty times what you would, Pip, in Alabama', the traumatised boy is told by Stubb. But poor Pip falls again and, tumbling into infinity, is nearly drowned, and almost left behind 'like a hurried traveller's trunk'.

'It was', Ishmael tells us, confidentially, 'a beautiful, bounteous, blue day'. The calm sea shines and sparkles, stretching away to the horizon. This is the deceptively-named Pacific, covering more of the earth than any one of its continents. We see, cinematically, Pip's head bobbing a mile away from the whale-boats which have abandoned him in their chase. He is at the corner of this image, like the downed winged boy in Breughel's painting, while the world goes about its business. He will be saved, but at the loss of his sanity. 'Blackness has its brilliancy', Ishmael observes, as he stares out under the tropical sun.

> The sea had jeeringly kept his finite body up, but drowned the infinite of his soul. Not drowned entirely, though. Rather carried alive down to wondrous depths, where strange shapes of the unwarped primal world glided to and from before his passive eyes; and the miser-merman, Wisdom, revealed his hoarded heaps; and among the joyous, heartless, ever-juvenile eternities, Pip saw the multitudinous, God-omniscient, coral insects, that out of the firmament of waters heaved the colossal orbs.

And so, says Ishmael, 'man's insanity is heaven's sense'.

*　*　*

Our whale falls to her transition, a being breaking boundaries, creating strange meetings. She is a mammal like us, breathing the same air, and yet she is able to occupy an alien deep in which we would perish. Is that why we feel a guilty connection to cetaceans, who left our venal land-bound life for the freedom of the ocean? Is this why we punish them for their impudence, for their rejection, these objects of unrequited love?

Once, on the sandy shores of Cape Cod, I lay alongside a dead dolphin that had stranded overnight on the beach. As I stroked her taut flanks and flukes, the shape of her hydrodynamic body seemed supremely suited to sliding through the water. Her presence, so close by, silently evoked the culture of her tribe: social, playful, deadly, designed, abiding. (Anyone wondering where the female is in Moby-Dick might consider that cetacean society is entirely matriarchal, and that the symbolic whale in Melville's book might be a she). When we project ourselves into their world, we imagine ourselves zipped up in dolphin wet suits – the whales we wish we once were. Around AD 180, the Greco-Roman poet Oppian declared that hunting 'the kingly dolphin' was immoral, on the grounds that they were once humans who had exchanged the land for the sea. 'But even now the righteous spirit of men in them preserves human thought and human deeds'. However, in the many times I have shared that inner space with living marine mammals, I have never touched them, nor they me. The gulf is too great. 'The eyes of an animal when they consider a man are attentive and wary', John Berger wrote. 'Man becomes aware of returning the look. The animal scrutinises him across a narrow abyss of non-comprehension'. We anthropomorphise to bring them under our control, to import them into our culture, ignorant as we are of theirs.

And isn't there something terrible and lonely about the fact that these creatures die at sea, with the darkness below them; the same darkness we all ultimately face? Stranded whales and dolphins may be seeking the shore as the last resort. As Andrew Brownlow, a Scottish scientist suggests, cetaceans 'will strand themselves when they are very weak because they don't want to drown'. To him, there seems to be 'something very deep in the terrestrial mammalian core that fires up when they are in extremis'. It is a compulsion that seems to be an act of both suicide and survival – an animal of the water, but breathing our air.

The sea is a mortal, eternal place; always the same, always changing. A vast volume, or a mere exchange of gases. Penetrable, permeable, but rejecting, resisting, defying human nominal dominion. For its inhabitants, water is the tangible means of connection, conducting sound rather than light. Our vaunted, human sense of sight is useless in those sunless depths. We cannot peer beneath what Melville called 'the ocean's skin'. Down there lies ninety per cent of the planet's biomass. We have yet to identify seventy-five per cent of the sea's species, which remain unseen, unknown.

And even the water itself has an age. At the National Oceanographic Centre in Southampton, a marine scientist tells me how the average age of the sea is four hundred years, and that some volumes of water in the ocean's benthic depths may be four thousand years old. Allied with the notion that some whales, such as the Arctic bowhead, can live for two hundred, perhaps three hundred years or more, our little lives fall into another context. In deep time, organisms, climate, life slows down.

Animate and inanimate, the sea is an accidental record of its own.

*   *   *

For Ellen, painting / penmanship / paper represents 'not so much a rule of letters but a kind of memory, time'. Mark-making seeks to stall time, in the way the deep ocean preserves it. Prospero asks Miranda: 'What seest thou else / In the dark backward and abysm of time?' And Melville tells us in his book, Mardi, that 'Backward or forward, eternity is the same; already we have been the nothing we dread to be'. There's a kind of collision of time and space in Ellen's work. As she says, 'Our effects on each other are still resonant and resonating. The whale was hunted to the brink of oblivion for the oil that fuels our velocities. But those velocities have created a need to mechanise ourselves, whether by conscription or quasi-consensual agreement'.

The Osedax series is accompanied – haunted, perhaps – by human figures. They evoke the 'isolatoes' of Moby-Dick, crews from islands and remote places: Cape Cod, the Azores, the Cape Verdes. The land does not own them any longer; they are given up to the sea and their duties, to a paradoxical freedom and serfdom.

'Do you think the archangel Gabriel thinks anything the less of me, because I promptly and respectfully obey that old hunks in that particular instance?' Ishmael asks. 'Who ain't a slave? Tell me that'.

Men sought the sea to escape, to become something else. 'Whale, human, worm, and water slowly turning back to space', Ellen writes. 'It is impossible to separate the whale from the shipwreck. The isolatoes are already bound to their fate at the bottom of the sea'.

'Is this maybe what you meant when you asked me about ships and civilisation in my paintings?' she asks me. In her work, Lips Sink, she refers to the ending of Moby-Dick. In the final, chaotic sequence, the book's unreliable narrator, Ishmael, survives the sinking of the whale-ship, the Pequod (named for a tribe of Native Americans driven to extinction). The vessel sinks, having been stove in by the great white whale that has already dragged his demented pursuer, Captain Ahab, down to the ocean depths. Ahab was a man in pursuit of an animal he had invested with a sense of evil for the damage it had done to his body, severing his leg (perhaps along with other body parts – as W.H. Auden wrote, 'the rare ambiguous monster that maimed his sex'). Yet what Melville tells us is that no animal demonstrates evil other than the human. In Moby-Dick, the human is the other.

In Ellen's hypnotic, swirling image, we are sucked down into the gyre of that green sea while Ishmael bobs to the surface with the froth, a frail body clinging to the empty coffin which was carved for his friend, Queequeg. At the beginning of the book, the two men had shared a New Bedford bed and proclaimed themselves married. Now Queequeg, who has drowned with the rest of the crew, inadvertently performs a last loyal act by providing Ishmael with a lifebuoy. 'I was thinking about Queequeg's coffin', Ellen tells me. 'His fever induced transcription of his own inky flesh, unknowable even to himself. The porous litho stone more alchemy than recipe'.

In the all-engulfing ocean and its cycles, all things come full circle. In Melville's final, elegiac work, Billy Budd, the Handsome Sailor (whom the author may have also intended, at one point, to be black) is hanged for his innocence, swinging as a 'pendant pearl' from the yardarm, before his body is consigned to the deep. '… Drop me down deep. / Fathoms down, fathoms down, how I'll dream fast asleep … / … I am sleepy, and the oozy weeds about me twist'. Dozing sensually with the fishes or negotiating the knowing nothingness of the ocean, Ellen Gallagher's work continues its terrible, beautiful dialogue with an element that gives and takes in turn: it is all the same, in the end. As Prospero says at the end of The Tempest, 'We are such stuff / As dreams are made on / and our little life / Is rounded with a sleep'.

* * *

Marconistraat, the street which runs along the wharves of Rotterdam, was named after a man who travelled across the Atlantic in his laboratory ship, Elettra, and believed that his radio receivers could listen to signals from outer space, as well as the cries of long-drowned sailors.

This morning, on the wharfside outside the studio, strips of 70mm aerial film are laid out in the sun. The light burns images into the Delft-blue cyanotype, infusing the celluloid – a material once made from the gelatine of hunted whales – with aquatic shapes, which slide through the film like animations, moving in and out of view, swirling down to the deep, or streaking across the sky like comets. Glowing with bioluminescence, they are fantastical x-rays of the sea, in the way that I once saw an x-ray of myself in which my bare bones looked as if they'd been picked clean by an osedax worm. We now know that chemosynthetic – as opposed to photosynthetic – organisms exist in the hydrothermal vents of the abyss. This is where life on earth began. And down there, in those dark, womb-like depths, far from the sun, the leviathan gently sways and settles into her little sleep.

[1] The Tempest draws on the story of the Sea Venture, wrecked on Bermuda in 1609 as it carried colonists from England to Virginia, an expedition partly funded by the Earl of Southampton, Shakespeare's 'Fair Youth' and probable lover. One of the crew, Stephen Hopkins, also from Southampton, returned to England and became one of the 'Strangers' on the Mayflower. His son, born on the voyage to Cape Cod, was named Oceanus.

[2] John Giono, French pacifist and author, was the first to translate Moby-Dick into French in 1939.

[3] In Aldous Huxley's dystopian Brave New World (1931), which takes its title from Miranda's naïve exclamation of wonder in The Tempest – 'How beauteous mankind is! Oh brave new world, / That has such people in't!' – members of the lower caste are referred to as 'octoroons', persons with one-eighth black blood.

*   *   *

Philip Hoare is the author of Leviathan, or The Whale and The Sea Inside. His new book, RISINGTIDEFALLINGSTAR, is published by University of Chicago Press and Fourth Estate.

With thanks to Jeroen Hoekendijk and Guido Keijl for sharing their knowledge of historic whale strandings in the Netherlands.

Editor's note: Philip Hoare's text has been preserved in United Kingdom Standard English for authorial integrity.

ELLEN GALLAGHER

Born in Providence, Rhode Island, 1965
Lives and works in Rotterdam, the Netherlands
and Brooklyn, New York

EDUCATION

Skowhegan School of Painting and Sculpture,
Skowhegan, Maine, 1993
School of the Museum of Fine Arts, Boston,
1992
Studio 70, Fort Thomas, Kentucky, 1989
SEA (Sea Education Association), Woods Hole,
Massachusetts, 1986–1987
Oberlin College, Oberlin, Ohio, 1982–1984

SOLO EXHIBITIONS

2017
Hauser & Wirth, Accidental Records,
Los Angeles

2014
Hauser & Wirth, New Work, London
Haus der Kunst, AxME, Munich
(Travelling Exhibition)

2013
Sara Hildén Art Museum, AxME, Tampere,
Finland (Travelling Exhibition)
SCAD Museum of Art, Ice or Salt, Savannah,
Georgia
New Museum, Don't Axe Me, New York
Tate Modern, AxME, London,
(Travelling Exhibition)

2011
Gagosian Gallery, Greasy, New York

2009
South London Gallery, An Experiment of
Unusual Opportunity, London

2007
Tate Liverpool, Coral Cities, Liverpool
(Travelling Exhibition)
Dublin City Gallery The Hugh Lane, Coral Cities,
Dublin (Travelling Exhibition)

2006
Hauser & Wirth London, Salt Eaters, London
Hauser & Wirth Zürich, DeLuxe, Zurich

2005
Freud Museum, Ellen Gallagher: Ichthyosaurus,
London
Museum of Contemporary Art, Ellen Gallagher:
Murmur and DeLuxe, Miami
Whitney Museum of American Art, Ellen
Gallagher: DeLuxe, New York

2004
Fruitmarket Gallery, Orbus, Edinburgh
Galerie im Taxispalais, Innsbruck

Gagosian Gallery, Ellen Gallagher: eXelento,
New York
Henry Art Gallery, Preserve / Murmur, Seattle

2003
Galerie Max Hetzler, Murmur, Berlin
Saint Louis Art Museum, Currents 88, St. Louis

2002
The Drawing Center, Preserve, New York
(Travelling Exhibition)
Museum of Contemporary Art, Watery Ecstatic,
Sydney (Travelling Exhibition)

2001
Gagosian Gallery, Blubber, New York
Institute of Contemporary Art, Watery Ecstatic,
Boston (Travelling Exhibition)
Des Moines Art Center, Preserve, Des Moines,
Iowa (Travelling Exhibition)
Yerba Buena Center for the Arts, Preserve,
San Francisco (Travelling Exhibition)

2000
Anthony d'Offay Gallery, London

1999
Mario Diacono Gallery, Boston
Galerie Max Hetzler, Berlin

1998
Gagosian Gallery, New York
IKON Gallery, Birmingham, England

1996
Anthony d'Offay Gallery, London
Mary Boone Gallery, New York

1994
Mario Diacono Gallery, Boston

SELECTED GROUP EXHIBITIONS

2017
Whitechapel Gallery, Material Desires, London
Contemporary Arts Centre, Prospect.4 New
Orleans, New Orleans
Centro de Arte Dos de Mayo, Elements of Vogue:
A Case Study in Radical Performance, Madrid
Museum of Contemporary Art, We Are
Everywhere, Chicago
Frans Hals Museum, A Global Table, Haarlem,
the Netherlands
Situations, The Tale, Torquay, England
The Walker Art Center, I am you, you are too,
Minneapolis
Carnegie Museum of Art, 20 / 20, Pittsburgh
Albright Knox Museum, Drawing: The Beginning
of Everything, Buffalo, New York
Royal Academy of Arts, Summer Exhibition,
London
ICF at Palazzo Pisani a Santa Marina, Diaspora
Platform, Venice
WIELS, The Absent Museum, Brussels
Sprüth Magers, Power, Los Angeles

Museum of Modern Art Warsaw, The Beguiling Siren is Thy Crest, **Warsaw**
Musée régional d'art contemporain, La vie aquatique, **Sérignan, France**

2016
The Broad, Creature, **Los Angeles**
Musée du quai Branly, The Color Line: African-American Artists and Civil Rights, **Paris**
International Print Center, Black Pulp!, **New York**
Bruce Museum, Her Crowd: New Art by Women from Our Neighbors' Private Collections, **Greenwich, Connecticut**
ICA Boston, First Light. The Barbara Lee Collection of Art by Women, **Boston**
University Art Museum, University at Albany, Future Perfect: Picturing the Anthropocene, **Albany, New York**
Pace Gallery, Blackness in Abstraction, **New York**
Denver Art Museum, Audacious: Contemporary Artists Speak Out, **Denver**
Vancouver Art Gallery, MashUp: The Birth of Modern Culture, **Vancouver, Canada**
32 Edgewood Avenue Gallery, Yale University School of Art, Black Pulp!, **New Haven**
Ackland Art Museum, Racial Violence and Resilience: Questions and Currents in African American Art, **Chapel Hill, North Carolina**

2015
S.M.A.K, The Bottom Line, **Ghent, Belgium**
Istanbul Modern, Saltwater. 14th Istanbul Biennial, **Istanbul**
The Hood Museum of Art, Dartmouth College, Collecting and Sharing: Trevor Fairbrother, John T. Kirk and the Hood Museum of Art, **Hanover, New Hampshire**
Magazin4, Das Als-ob-Prinzip, **Bregenz, Austria**
Haus der Kunst, Random Sampling – Painting from the Goetz Collection, **Munich**
Goodman Gallery, Speaking Back, **Cape Town**
La Biennale di Venezia, 56th International Art Exhibition, All the World's Futures, **Venice**
SEASpace Gallery, Cape Whale: A New Look Through Art, Science and Culture, **Provincetown, Massachusetts**
Montclair Art Museum, Come as You Are. Art of the 1990s, **Montclair, New Jersey**
Addison Gallery of American Art, Phillips Academy, Collection Intervention: Ellen Gallagher's DeLuxe, **Andover, Massachusetts**
The New Art Gallery Walsall, FOUND, **Walsall, England**
Johnson Museum of Art, Cornell University, This Is No Less Curious: Journeys Through the Collection, **Ithaca, New York**
MK Gallery, How to Construct a Time Machine, **Milton Keynes, England**

2014
The Studio Museum in Harlem, Speaking of People: Ebony, Jet and Contemporary Art, **New York**
Whitney Museum of American Art, Shaping a Collection. Five Decades of Gifts, **New York**

2013
The Studio Museum in Harlem, The Shadows Took Shape, **New York**
FLAG Art Foundation, FLAG's 5th Anniversary Group Exhibition, **New York**

2012
Palais de Tokyo, La Triennale, **Paris, France**
MoMA Museum of Modern Art, Printin', **New York**
MoMA Museum of Modern Art, Print / Out, **New York**
Museum voor Moderne Kunst, Six Yards. Guaranteed Dutch Design, **Arnhem, the Netherlands**

2010
Centro Galego de Arte Contemporánea, Afro Modern: Journeys through the Black Atlantic, **Santiago de Compostela, Spain (Travelling Exhibition)**
La Cinémathèque française, Brune / Blonde. Une exposition Arts et Cinéma, **Paris**
MoMA Museum of Modern Art, On Line: Drawing Through the Twentieth Century, **New York**
Whitney Museum of American Art, Whitney Biennial, **New York**
Tate Liverpool, Afro Modern: Journey through the Black Atlantic, **Liverpool, England (Travelling Exhibition)**
Whitney Museum of American Art, Collecting Biennials, **New York**

2009
Albright-Knox Art Gallery, Topographies, **Buffalo, New York**
Whitney Museum of American Art, A Few Frames: Photography and the Contact Sheet, **New York**
Centre Georges Pompidou, elles@centrepompidou, **Paris (Travelling Exhibition)**
MoMA Museum of Modern Art, Paper: Pressed, Stained, Slashed, Folded, **New York**

2008
Moderna Museet, Eclipse. Art in a Dark Age, **Stockholm**

2007
Museum of Contemporary Art, Collection Highlights, **Chicago**
Thomas Dane Gallery, Very Abstract and Hyper Figurative, **London**
MoMA Museum of Modern Art, Comic Abstraction, **New York**
The Model Arts Gallery & Niland Gallery, The Secret Theory of Drawing, **Sligo, Ireland (Travelling Exhibition)**
Tate Modern, Passages from History, **London**

2006
ICA – Institute of Contemporary Arts, Alien Nation, **London (Travelling Exhibition)**
Walker Art Center, Heart of Darkness,

Minneapolis
Villa Manin Centre for Contemporary Art, Infinite Painting. Contemporary Painting and Global Realism, **Codroipo, Italy**
Whitney Museum of American Art, Skin is a Language, **New York**

2005
Yerba Buena Center for the Arts, Black Panther Rank and File, **San Francisco**
Contemporary Arts Museum, Double Consciousness: Black Conceptual Art Since 1970, **Houston**

2004
Fondazione Sandretto Re Rebaudengo, Non Toccare la Donna Bianca, **Turin**
SITE Santa Fe's Fifth International Biennial, Disparities and Deformations: Our Grotesque, **Santa Fe**

2003
MoMA Museum of Modern Art, Artist's Choice: Mona Hatoum, Here is elsewhere, **New York**
The Studio Museum in Harlem, Black Belt, **New York**
MoMA Museum of Modern Art, Stranger in the Village, **New York**
La Biennale di Venezia, 50th International Art Exhibition, Dreams and Conflicts. The Dictatorship of the Viewer, **Venice**

2002
Jack S. Blanton Museum of Art, University of Texas at Austin, Cartoon Noir: Contemporary Investigations, **Austin**

2001
Sammlung Goetz, The Mystery of Painting, **Munich**

2000
P.S.1 Contemporary Art Center in collaboration with MoMA Museum of Modern Art, Greater New York: New Art in New York Now, **New York**
IMMA Irish Museum of Modern Art, Half Dust, **Dublin**

1999
École Nationale Supérieure des Beaux-Arts, (Corps) Social, **Paris**

1998
Museo de la Ciudad de México, Cinco continentes y una ciudad, **Mexico City**

1997
IMMA Irish Museum of Modern Art, Projects, **Dublin**
Art Gallery of Western Australia, Inside the Visible, **Perth (Travelling Exhibition)**

1996
National Museum of Women in Arts, Inside the Visible, **Washington D.C. (Travelling Exhibition)**
Institute of Contemporary Art, Inside the Visible, **Boston (Travelling Exhibition)**
Whitechapel Art Gallery, Inside the Visible, **London (Travelling Exhibition)**

1995
Whitney Museum of American Art, 1995 Biennial Exhibition, **New York**

PUBLIC COLLECTIONS

Albright-Knox Art Gallery, Buffalo, New York
Bowes Foundation, San Francisco
Broad Family Foundation, Los Angeles
Centre Georges Pompidou, Paris
Denver Art Museum, Denver
Des Moines Art Center, Des Moines, Iowa
ICA Boston, Boston
Irish Museum of Modern Art – IMMA, Dublin
Jack S. Blanton Museum of Art, Austin
Joslyn Museum of Art, Omaha, Nebraska
Moderna Museet, Stockholm
Museum of Contemporary Art, Chicago
Museum of Contemporary Art, Los Angeles
Museum of Fine Arts, Boston
Philadelphia Museum of Art, Philadelphia
Rose Art Museum, Brandeis University, Waltham, Massachusetts
Saint Louis Art Museum, Saint Louis
Sammlung Goetz, Munich
San Francisco Museum of Modern Art, San Francisco
Sara Hildén Art Museum, Tampere, Finland
Seattle Art Museum, Seattle, Washington
The Metropolitan Museum of Art, New York
The Museum of Modern Art, New York
The Studio Museum in Harlem, New York
Art Institute of Chicago, Chicago
Tate, London, England
Walker Art Center, Minneapolis
Whitney Museum of American Art, New York

Published on the occasion of the exhibition
Ellen Gallagher: Accidental Records
Hauser & Wirth, Los Angeles
4 November 2017–28 January 2018

Artist book conceived by Ellen Gallagher

Editorial Coordination
Stefan Zebrowski-Rubin

Project Coordination
Soraya Rodriguez, Neil Wenman

Book design and typography
Kellenberger–White

Copy editing and proofreading
Emma Capps

Pre-press and printed by
Unicum | Gianotten Printed Media

Ellen Gallagher: Accidental Records
© 2017 Hauser & Wirth Publishers
www.hauserwirth.com

Photo Credits
For images on p. 5: Baschz Leeft; p. 6: Jan
Oosterhuis; pp. 11, 12 and 82: Ellen Gallagher;
pp. 13–15, 17–22: Tom Powel Imaging; pp. 27–29:
Alex Delfanne; p. 32 (bottom): Barbora Gerny;
pp. 43–48, 96–100: Philippe Vogelenzang,
courtesy HALAL; pp. 53, 55–59, 61–65, 67–71,
78: Ernst Moritz; p. 80 (bottom): Jeroen
Hoekendijk; p. 85: Todd White Art Photography.

For artwork by Henri Matisse (p. 32): Henri
Matisse (French, 1869–1954), Artist and Model
Reflected in a Mirror, 1937. Pen and black ink,
sheet: 612 × 415 mm. (24 ⅛ × 16 ⁵⁄₁₆ in). The
Baltimore Museum of Art: The Cone Collection,
formed by Dr. Claribel Cone and Miss Etta Cone
of Baltimore, Maryland, BMA 1950.12.51.
Photo: Mitro Hood. Courtesy The Baltimore
Museum of Art.

For images on pp. 17–22: Courtesy Gagosian;
p. 32 (photograph of Matisse): © 2017 Digital
image: The Museum of Modern Art, New York/
Scala, Florence; p. 35 (Baumann): © 2017
Christie's Images, London/Scala, Florence;
p. 35 (Ingres): © 2017 A. Dagli Orti/Scala,
Florence; p. 35 (Picasso): © 2017 Photo Josse/
Scala, Florence; p. 35 (O'Grady): © 2017 Lorraine
O'Grady/Artists Rights Society (ARS),
New York. Courtesy Alexander Gray Associates,
New York; p. 79: © Trustees of the British
Museum; p. 81: © 2017 The Fitzwilliam Museum,
Cambridge/Scala, Florence.

Every effort has been made to trace copyright
ownership and to obtain reproduction
permissions. Corrections brought to the
publisher's attention will be incorporated in
future reprints or editions of this book.

Cataloguing-in-Publication Data is available
from the Library of Congress.

Available in North America through
ARTBOOK | D.A.P.
75 Broad Street, Suite 630
New York, NY 10004
Tel 212 627 1999
Fax 212 627 9484

ISBN: 978-3-906915-10-4

Printed and bound in the Netherlands

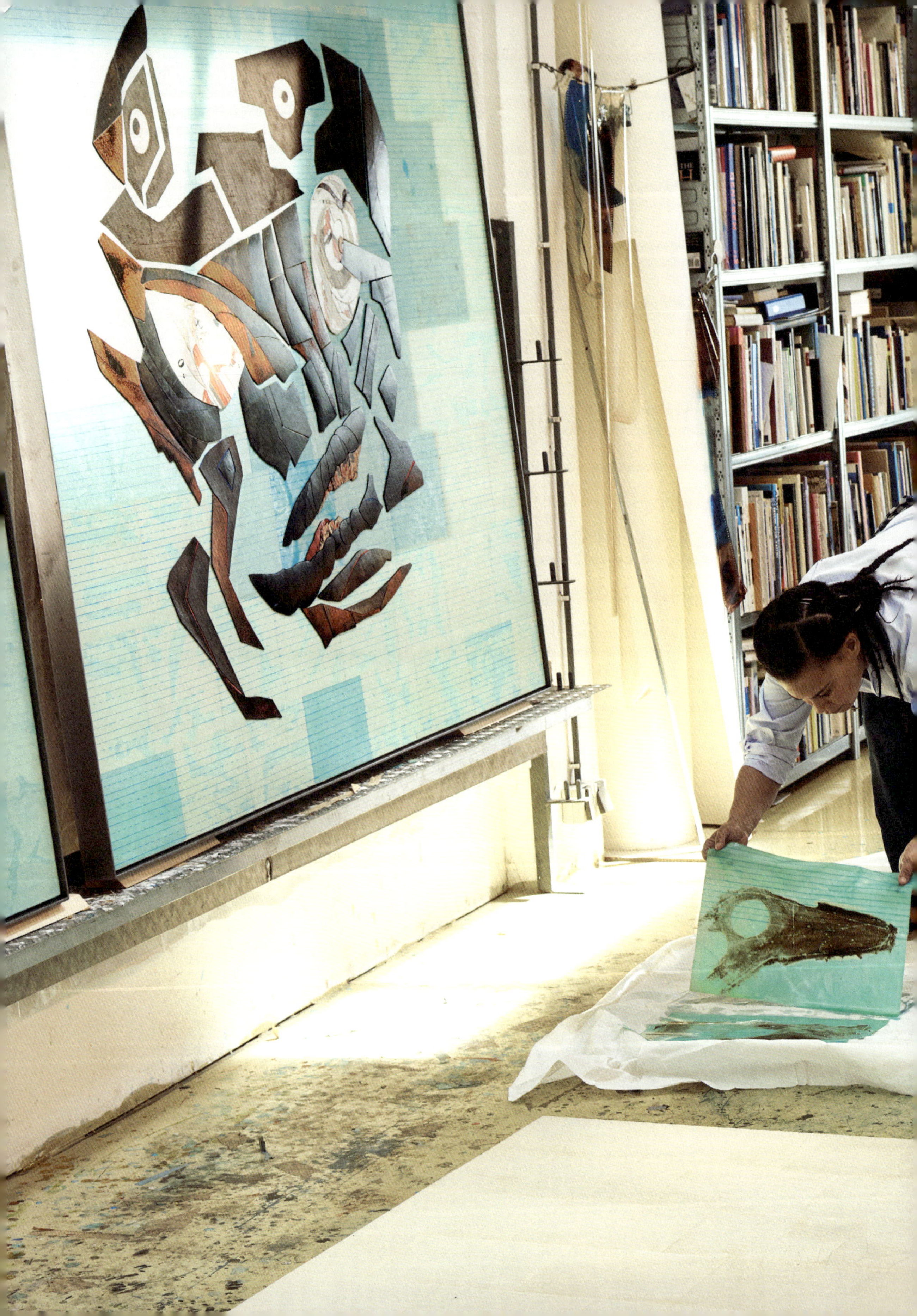